SCOTT FORESMAN

Art

Robyn Montana Turner, Ph.D.
Program Author

PEARSON

Scott
Foresman

Editorial Offices: Glenview, Illinois • Parsippany, New Jersey • New York, New York

Sales Offices: Parsippany, New Jersey • Duluth, Georgia • Glenview, Illinois • Coppell, Texas • Ontario, California • Mesa, Arizona

1 2 3 4 5 6 7 8 9 10 V057 13 12 11 10 09 08 07 06 05 04

Program Consultants

Christopher Adejumo, Ph.D.
Associate Professor
Visual Art Studies
University of Texas
Austin, Texas

Doug Blandy, Ph.D.
Professor and Director
Arts and Administration Program
Institute for Community Arts and Studies
University of Oregon
Eugene, Oregon

Rebecca Brooks, Ph.D.
Professor
Department of Art and Art History
University of Texas
Austin, Texas

Sara A. Chapman, Ed.D.
Director of Fine Arts
Alief Independent School District
Houston, Texas

James Clarke, M.Ed.
Executive Director
Texas Coalition for Quality Arts Education
Houston, Texas

Georgia Collins, Ph.D.
Professor Emeritus
College of Fine Arts
University of Kentucky
Lexington, Kentucky

Deborah Cooper, M.Ed.
Coordinating Director of Arts Education
Curriculum and Instruction
Charlotte-Mecklenburg Schools
Charlotte, North Carolina

Sandra M. Epps, Ph.D.
Multicultural Art Education Consultant
New York, New York

Mary Jo Gardere
Multi-Arts Specialist
Eladio Martinez Learning Center
Dallas, Texas

Carlos G. Gómez, M.F.A.
Professor of Fine Art
University of Texas at Brownsville
and Texas Southmost College
Brownsville, Texas

Kristina Lamour, M.F.A.
Assistant Professor
The Art Institute of Boston
at Lesley University
Boston, Massachusetts

Melinda M. Mayer, Ph.D.
Assistant Professor
School of Visual Arts
University of North Texas
Denton, Texas

Reviewers

Studio Reviewers

Judy Abbott, *Art Educator*
Allison Elementary School
Austin Independent School
District
Austin, Texas

Lin Altman, *Art Educator*
Cedar Creek Elementary
School
Eanes Independent School
District
Austin, Texas

Geral T. Butler, *Art Educator*
(Retired)
Heritage High School
Lynchburg City Schools
Lynchburg, Virginia

Dale Case, *Elementary Principal*
Fox Meadow Elementary
School
Nettleton School District
Jonesboro, Arkansas

Deborah McLouth, *Art Educator*
Zavala Elementary School
Austin Independent School
District
Austin, Texas

Patricia Newman, *Art Educator*
Saint Francis Xavier School
Archdiocese of Chicago
La Grange, Illinois

Nancy Sass, *Art Educator*
Cambridge Elementary
School
Alamo Heights Independent
School District
San Antonio, Texas

Sue Spiva Telle, *Art Educator*
Woodridge Elementary
School
Alamo Heights Independent
School District
San Antonio, Texas

Cari Washburn, *Art Educator*
Great Oaks Elementary
School
Round Rock Independent
School District
Round Rock, Texas

Critic Readers

Celeste Anderson
Roosevelt Elementary School
Nampa, Idaho

Mary Jo Burkwocz
Wilson Elementary School
Janesville, Wisconsin

Mary Jane Cahalan
Mitzi Bond Elementary
School
El Paso, Texas

Cindy Collar
Cloverleaf Elementary School
Cartersville, Georgia

Yvonne Days
St. Louis Public Schools
St. Louis, Missouri

Shirley Dickey
Creative Art Magnet School
Houston, Texas

Ray Durkee
Charlotte Performing Arts
Center
Punta Gorda, Florida

Sue Flores-Minick
Bryker Woods Elementary
School
Austin, Texas

Alicia Lewis
Stevens Elementary School
Houston, Texas

Denise Jennings
Fulton County Schools
Atlanta, Georgia

James Miller
Margo Elementary School
Weslaco, Texas

Marta Olson
Seattle Public Schools
Seattle, Washington

Judy Preble
Florence Avenue School
Irvington, New Jersey

Tonya Roberson
Oleson Elementary School
Houston, Texas

Andrew Southwick
Edgewood Independent
School District
San Antonio, Texas

Nita Ulaszek
Audelia Creek Elementary
School
Dallas, Texas

Tessie Varthas
Office of Creative and
Public Art
Philadelphia, Pennsylvania

Penelope Venola
Spurgeon Intermediate
School
Santa Ana, California

Elizabeth Willett
Art Specialist
Fort Worth, Texas

Contents

Unit 1

Art in Your World 16

Grant Wood.
American Gothic,
1930.

Unit 2

Cultural Expressions 50

Frida Kahlo. *Long LIve Life (Viva la vida),* 1954.

1

Unit 3

Expression in Art 84

David Gilhooly. *Frog Sandwich,* 1990.

Unit 4

Creative Expression 118

Thana Lauhakaikal.
Celebration,
1983–1985.

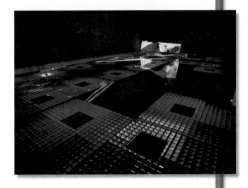

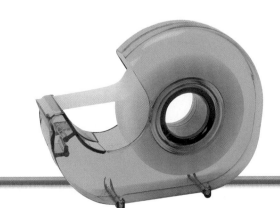

Unit 5

Art, Old and New 152

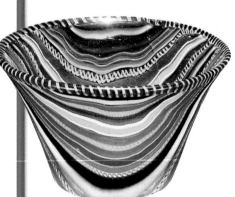

Artist unknown.
Ribbon Glass Cup,
ca. A.D. 1st century.

Unit 6

An Assortment of Art..........186

David Moctezuma.
Alebreje, 2003.

Start with Art

What is art? Is it a beautiful painting? Is it a colorful garden? Is it a sparkling item of jewelry? Art is all these things and so much more.

Art is everywhere. You can experience art every day. It is also important to understand art.

Ask yourself these questions.
Who makes art?
What is art?
Where is art made?
Why do artists make art?
How do artists make art?

These questions can help you learn about art. They can also help you form conclusions about what you see.

This book explores these questions and more. It talks about the nature of art. It also shows you how to create your own artworks.

You are an artist. Look for art all around you. You may find new ways to express your ideas and feelings.

Vincent van Gogh. *Irises,* 1889. Oil on canvas, 28 by 36⅝ inches. The J. Paul Getty Museum, Los Angeles.

Look in your kitchen for artworks. What other artworks can you find in your home?

Artist unknown. *Gold Stag,* 6th-5th century B.C. Republic of Tuva, Russia.

Your Art Words

To understand art, it is important to understand the language of art. Your book contains many art words. They are shown in **yellow.** These words help artists talk about art.

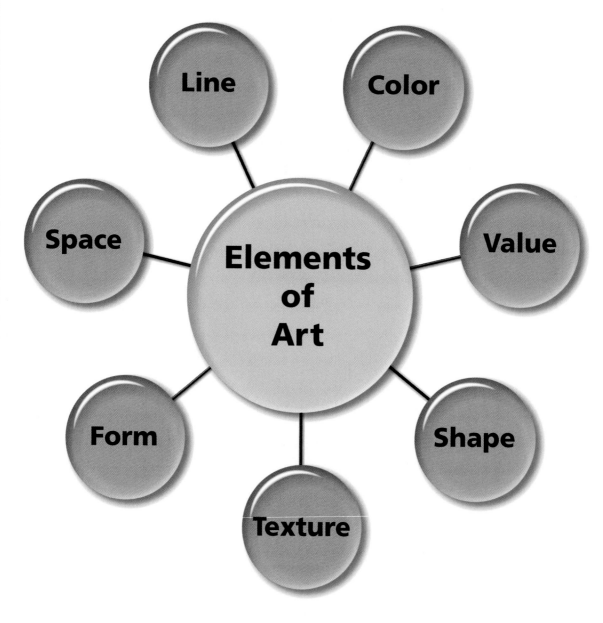

These art words name parts of an artwork.

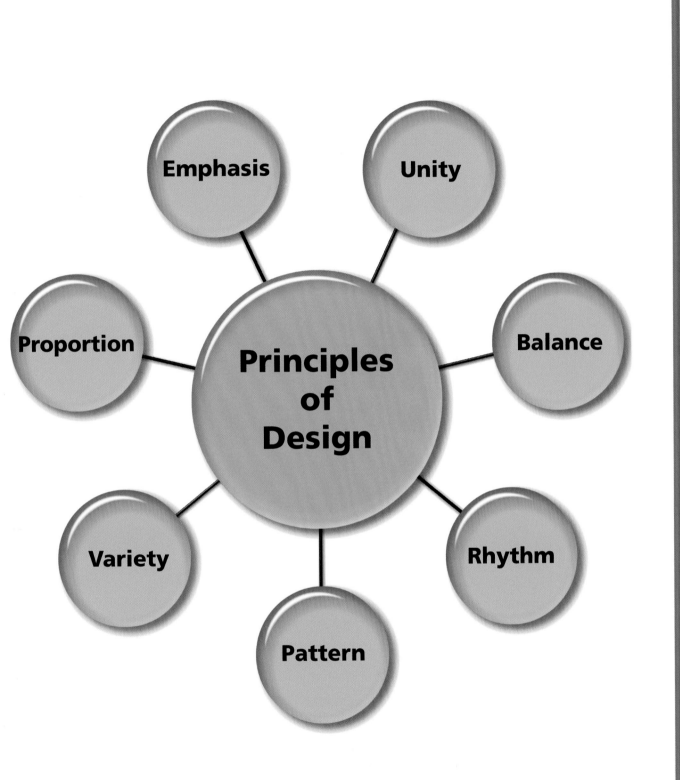

These art words tell how an artwork is put together.

William H. Johnson. *Chalet in the Mountains*, ca. 1938. Oil on burlap, 28½ by 35⅛ inches. Smithsonian American Art Museum, Washington, D.C.

Visit a Museum

Art museums are places that collect and display artworks. You can see artworks like this at an art museum.

Many people work in art museums. One such person is the curator. A **curator** is an art expert who collects and takes care of artworks. The curator also decides where to place the artworks.

Another person you may see at an art museum is a docent. **Docents** greet visitors and show them around the museum. They also provide information about the art and artists. They can answer questions to help you better understand the art.

What questions would you ask about this artwork?

Art Tools

Artists use tools to make their artworks. Different types of tools are used to create different types of art. Think about some of the art tools you would like to explore as you make your own artwork.

Chalk pastels and artists' pencils can be used for drawing.

Artists often experiment with many types of paint-brushes and other tools when painting.

These tools are used to make beautiful mosaic designs.

Ink, paint, sponges, and a roller called a brayer, are tools used in printmaking.

When artists make clay sculptures, they use some of these tools.

Photography is the art of taking pictures. The most important tools for photography are a camera and film.

Make a Portfolio

Artists often keep their artworks in a portfolio. You can store your flat artwork in a portfolio too. Follow these steps to make a portfolio. Use it to share your artworks with others.

1 Use two sheets of poster board. Write your name across the top of one sheet.

2 Place one sheet over the other. Be sure your name is on the front.

3 Tape the bottom and sides of your portfolio.

4 Use colored markers to decorate your portfolio.

Make a Sketchbook Journal

Many artists plan by drawing sketches. Sketches can help them remember what they have seen or imagined. Artists also record their thoughts and feelings with their sketches.

A sketchbook is a special tool. In it, artists can draw, paint, and even write their ideas. Later, they can use their sketches as a starting place for a larger artwork.

Look at this sketch by Pablo Picasso. Do you make sketches like this?

Pablo Picasso. *Don Quijote,* 1955. Pen and Ink sketch. Private collection.

Follow these steps to make a Sketchbook Journal.

1 Fold eight sheets of drawing paper in half.

2 Staple the sheets together along the fold.

3 Fold and staple a construction paper cover.

4 Decorate the cover. Write your name on it.

Claude Monet. (Detail) *Waterlilies: Green Reflections,* 1916–1923. Detail of the far left side, Room 1. Musée de l'Orangerie, Paris, France.

Art in Your World

Artists take inspiration from their environments. They create artworks using line, shape, color, value, texture, form, and space. These are the **elements of art.** The **principles of design,** or unity, variety, emphasis, balance, proportion, pattern, and rhythm, help artists to communicate feelings and ideas. How did Monet communicate his feelings in *Waterlilies*?

Meet the Artist

Artist Claude Monet belonged to a group of painters called Impressionists. Monet often painted outdoors. He is well known for his colorful paintings of water lilies. For many years, Monet had problems with his sight, yet he continued to paint. You will see another painting by Monet later in this unit.

Claude Monet. *Self-Portrait,* 1917.

Line

If you move your pencil point along a surface, you form a **line.** A line in an artwork is a continuous mark made on a surface by a tool. Artists use lines in their artworks to express many ideas.

Grant Wood. *American Gothic,* 1930. Oil on beaver board, 29¾ by 25 inches. The Art Institute of Chicago and VAGA, New York. Friends of American Art Collection, image © 1996 The Art Institute of Chicago, 1930.934. All rights reserved. Photograph © 1996, The Art Institute of Chicago.

Types of Lines

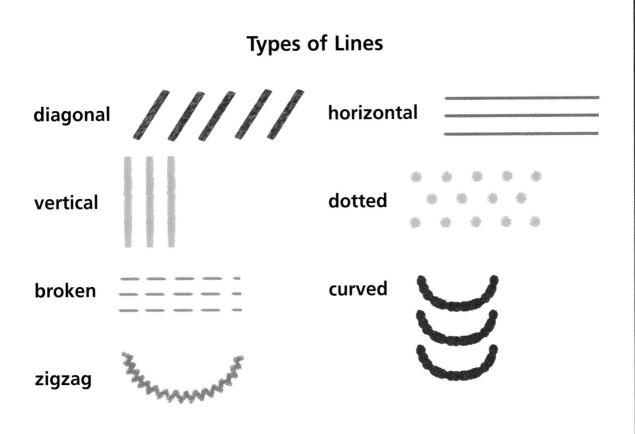

diagonal

horizontal

vertical

dotted

broken

curved

zigzag

Lines drawn in different ways suggest different kinds of movement, ideas, or feelings. A **horizontal** line may make you feel calm. A **vertical** line may show strength. **Diagonal** lines may suggest movement or tension. Notice the different kinds of lines on this page. How many of these lines can you find in Grant Wood's painting?

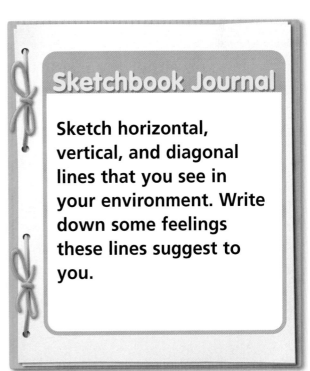

Sketchbook Journal

Sketch horizontal, vertical, and diagonal lines that you see in your environment. Write down some feelings these lines suggest to you.

Studio 1

Design a New School

What features would you include in the perfect school? Think about what you want in the building, and then follow these steps.

1 Imagine either the inside or the outside of your new school.

 2 Draw your school design.

Technique Tip

Try using a dull pencil and a sharp pencil to create different effects with your lines.

3 As you draw, use a variety of lines. How many kinds can you include?

4 Add some finishing touches to your drawing.

Think Like an Artist

Describe the different lines you used in your drawing. What does each kind communicate?

See and Imagine Lines

These paintings have the same subject—a group of men. The **subject** of an artwork is what the artwork is about, such as an animal, object, or scene. Look closely at the **details.** Studying these small parts of an artwork will help you know more about the painting.

Henri Rousseau. *Les joueurs de football (The Football Players),* 1908. Oil on canvas, 39½ by 31⅝ inches. The Solomon R. Guggenheim Museum, New York. © The Solomon R. Guggenheim Foundation, New York (FN 60.1583). Photograph by David Heald.

Katsushika Hokusai. *Six Master Poets,* Edo period (Tokugawa). Ink and color on paper, 13 by 22 inches. The Freer Gallery of Art, Smithsonian Institution, Washington, D.C.

Artists use two kinds of lines. Look at the stripes on the shirts of Rousseau's football players. A line you can see is called an **actual line.** Lines that are imagined but not actually seen are **implied lines.** With your fingers, follow a line from the eyes of one poet to another in the artwork by Hokusai. You can imagine the line, but you cannot see it. Describe other actual and implied lines in both paintings.

Sketchbook Journal

Think about a game or activity that you enjoy. Make a sketch, including both actual and implied lines. Each kind of line is important to your sketch. Write down why this is so.

Studio 2

Make Lines

Follow these steps to experiment with both actual and implied lines.

1 Draw a design on colored paper using glue. Leave some open spaces.

2 Cut strings and lay them along the glue lines.

Technique Tip

Leave some glue lines uncovered where a viewer could imagine implied lines that connect one string to another.

3 Repeat the same design on another sheet of paper, but use crayons.

4 Have a friend locate actual and implied lines in both artworks.

Think Like an Artist

Did your friend see the same implied lines that you did? Explain why or why not.

Shape

What shapes do you notice in this painting? A **shape** in a painting is a flat area, such as a circle or square. It has height and width but not depth.

Marianne von Werefkin. *The Washerwomen,* 1908–1909. Tempera on paper mounted on board, 20 by 25 inches. Städtische Galerie im Lenbachhaus, Munich, Germany.

Shapes

Geometric Shapes

Organic Shapes

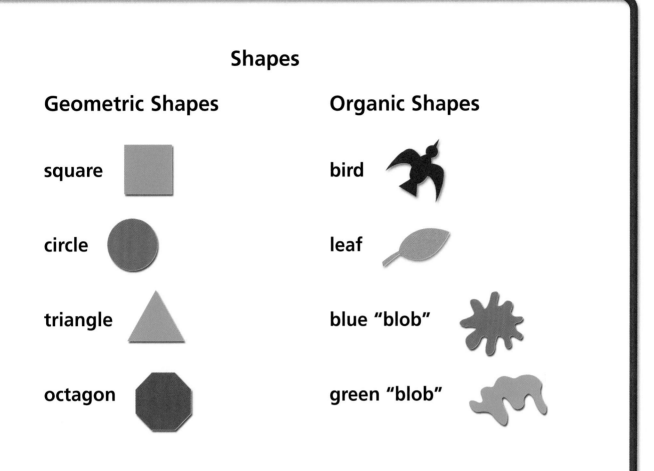

square

circle

triangle

octagon

bird

leaf

blue "blob"

green "blob"

Some shapes in *The Washerwomen* look like circles, triangles, squares, and other **geometric shapes** you have explored in math. Often, human-made objects have geometric shapes. *The Washerwomen* also includes **organic shapes.** These shapes look like objects you see in nature, such as clouds or puddles. What geometric and organic shapes can you find in the painting?

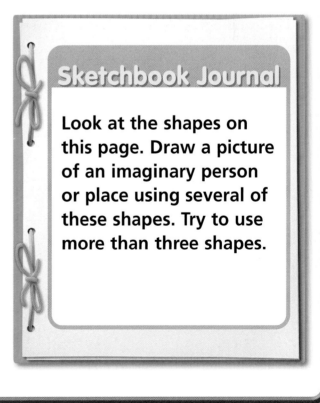

Sketchbook Journal

Look at the shapes on this page. Draw a picture of an imaginary person or place using several of these shapes. Try to use more than three shapes.

Create a Shape Collage

Imagine a scene from a familiar environment. Show the scene in a collage of shapes.

 1 Draw some organic and geometric shapes for your scene.

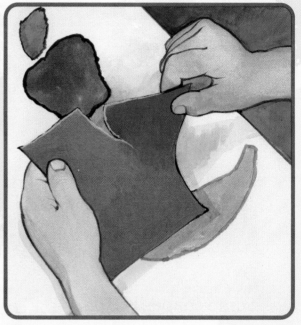

2 Tear similar shapes from colored paper.

Technique Tip

Add interest by varying the edges of your paper. Tear to make rough edges. For a smooth edge, fold paper first, and tear on the fold.

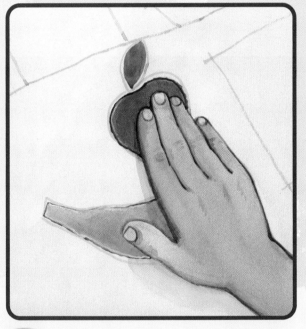

3 Glue the torn paper shapes into place on your sketch.

4 Draw or paint more shapes to complete your collage.

Think Like an Artist

Did your organic and geometric shapes turn out the way you planned? Would you make any changes? Why or why not?

Churches

Artists can choose from many different subjects for their paintings. Monet sometimes chose buildings as his subjects. This painting shows a church in France. How does this church differ from the one by Georgia O'Keeffe on the next page?

Claude Monet. *Rouen Cathedral,* 1894. Oil on canvas, 39¼ by 25⅞ inches. The Metropolitan Museum of Art, New York.

Georgia O'Keeffe. *Ranchos Church–Taos,* 1930. Oil on canvas, 24¼ by 36 inches. Courtesy of Amon Carter Museum, Ft. Worth, Texas. © 1997 The Georgia O'Keeffe Foundation/Artists Rights Society (ARS), New York.

Georgia O'Keeffe created this painting of an adobe church in New Mexico.

Think about how these paintings are alike and how they are different. How many different kinds of lines can you find? Are the shapes organic or geometric? Explain your answer.

Research

The Impressionist painters were named after Monet's painting, *Impression: Sunrise*. Find it in an art book or encyclopedia.

Texture

When you touch a surface or an object, it might feel smooth, bumpy, soft, hard, or sticky. The way a surface or object feels is its **texture.** Texture is an element of art.

Frank Romero. *Scamp in the Snow,* 1995. Oil on paper, 17 by 24 inches. Courtesy of Frank Romero.

These glasses show visual texture.

If you touched a real cat you could feel its **tactile texture.** Many artworks show **visual texture.** This is texture that you see rather than feel.

The visual texture of the glasses in the photograph is shiny. If you could touch the glasses, their tactile texture would be smooth. What textures do you see in *Scamp in the Snow?*

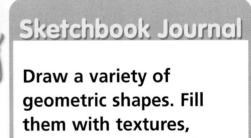

Sketchbook Journal

Draw a variety of geometric shapes. Fill them with textures, such as rough, pebbly, and lumpy. Use your imagination to add more textures to your drawing.

Studio 4

Rub Textures

Use a mix of shapes and textures to make a texture rubbing.

1 Draw your favorite animal on the paper.

2 Add large shapes that might appear in the animal's environment.

Technique Tip

Make test rubbings of different textures on scrap paper before adding them to your picture.

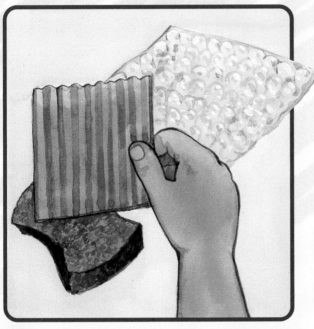

 3 Rub crayons over a different texture for each part of the picture.

4 Cover the entire picture with one color of thinned tempera.

Think Like an Artist

If you could do the project again, what would you do differently? How did the rubbing help to describe your animal?

Space and Distance

Look around and notice how objects that are far away appear smaller than those that are close. To show this in artworks, many artists use **space,** the area within and around shapes. This element helps artists show distance in artworks.

Clara McDonald Williamson. *The Old Chisholm Trail,* 1952. Oil on panel, 24 by 36½ inches. The Roland P. Murdock Collection, Wichita Art Museum, Wichita, Kansas.

Objects in the foreground of the picture appear larger than those in the background.

What objects in this photograph seem closer to the viewer? The part of an artwork that seems nearest is the **foreground. Background** is the part that seems farthest away. **Middle ground** is the area in between. Point to objects in the painting and photograph that are in the foreground, middle ground, or background. Notice how the cattle in the foreground cover, or **overlap,** one another.

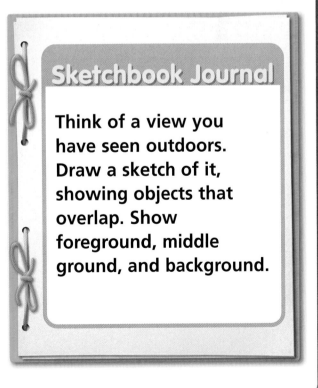

Sketchbook Journal

Think of a view you have seen outdoors. Draw a sketch of it, showing objects that overlap. Show foreground, middle ground, and background.

Studio 5

Make a Nature Scene

Make some objects appear farther away than others in a nature scene.

1 Draw a scene that has foreground, middle ground, and background.

2 Choose different colors for the foreground, middle ground, and background.

Technique Tip

Overlap small objects in the background first. Make objects gradually larger in the middle ground and foreground.

3 Overlap objects to show depth.

4 Add details to the objects in the foreground.

Think Like an Artist

Ask a friend to identify the foreground, middle ground, and background of your drawing.

Artists See Spaces

People see spaces in artworks in different ways. In the artwork on this page, most people see the leaf shape first. This area is called **positive space.** The area around the positive space is called **negative space.**

Rupert García. *Maguey de la Vida,* 1973. Color screenprint, 18⅔ by 24⅞ inches. Fine Arts Museums of San Francisco, gift of Mr. and Mrs. Robert Marcus, 1990.1.116.

What attracts your eye in this image?

Negative space serves as contrast. It helps you see the positive space. Both positive and negative spaces are parts of the **composition,** or the whole artwork.

Point to the positive space in the picture on this page. Positive space has outlines, edges, or colors that attract your eye. Now look at the negative space in García's artwork. How did he make the positive space stand out?

Art in My World

Find a family photo. It might be of your last birthday or from a family trip. Identify the positive and negative space in the picture.

Draw a Cover Design

Plan a composition for a CD or DVD cover. How will you show positive and negative space? Follow these steps.

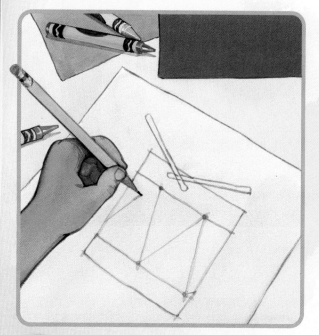

1 Use a pencil to draw the main shape or image for your CD or DVD cover.

2 Use swirly lines to make interesting shapes on another sheet of paper.

Technique Tip

Choose colors to help you show positive space. Choose other colors to help you show negative space.

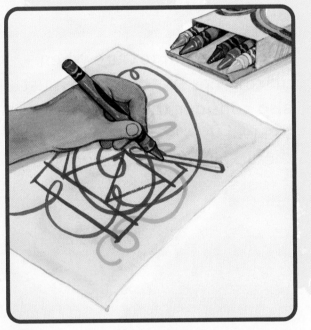

3 Draw the main shape or image for your cover.

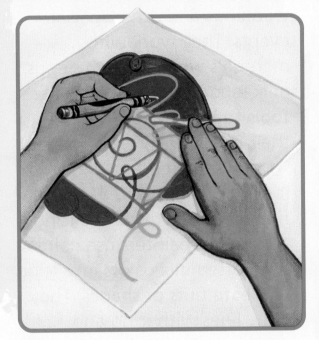

4 Color in dark shapes next to light ones to make a visual puzzle.

Think Like an Artist

Do you think your cover design will make people want to buy the CD or DVD? Why or why not?

Cake Designs

Toba Garrett, right, teaches cake design at the Institute of Culinary Education in New York.

Chef Toba Garrett combines food and art to express herself. She is a cake designer. Cake designers plan cakes for weddings and other special events. They work with materials we eat, such as eggs, milk, and sugar. They also use tools to help them add icing to their cakes.

Icing is made from sugar. It can be thin, thick, fluffy, or firm. Cake designers use icing almost like painters use paints. They often mix colors into icing to create tints or shades. They draw lines with icing and experiment with shapes.

Garrett begins her cake designs with a pencil and sketchbook. She considers color, line, and texture when making her sketches. She must also consider the ingredients she will use. A great cake should always taste as good as it looks.

Cake designers use tools such as this spatula and icing bag to add texture to their cakes.

What colors, lines, and textures has Garrett added to this cake?

Make an Etching

Show your interest in a hobby or sport. Use what you know about line, shape, texture, and space.

1

Color many shapes with bright oil pastels. Press hard and fill the whole paper.

2

Color over the paper again with black crayon or oil pastel. Press hard.

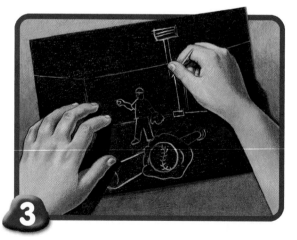

3

Use a toothpick to draw objects. Include foreground, middle ground, and background.

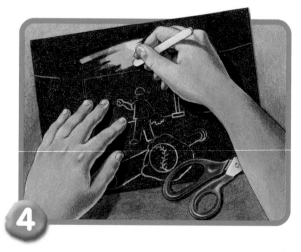

4

Use a craft stick and other tools to scratch away the negative space.

Gavin, Age 9. *Tubing at the Lake.* Crayon.

Morgan, Age 9. *Fishing.* Crayon.

Look at how these students etched scenes showing their favorite hobbies or sports.

Share Your Art

1. What kinds of lines and shapes did you use? What kinds of texture?

2. Where are the foreground, middle ground, and background in your artwork?

Think About Art

Read the art words. Then point to a picture that matches each word. Explain how the picture illustrates what the word means.

background   geometric shape   organic shape
diagonal line   horizontal line   subject
foreground   negative space   texture

Write About Art

Look around your immediate environment. How do the lines, shapes, and textures affect how people might feel in that place? Write about them.

Talk About Art

- Look through your portfolio.
- Choose an artwork that best shows a variety of lines and shapes.
- Tell a friend about the lines and shapes.
- Explain what you used to make this artwork.

Gabriele Münter. *The Russian House (Das Russen-Haus),* 1931. Oil on canvas, 16¾ by 22½ inches. Städtische Galerie im Lenbachhaus, Munich, Germany.

Put It All Together

1. Describe the subject of the painting. What elements of art did the artist use to show the subject?

2. How did the artist show foreground, middle ground, and background? How did she show positive and negative space?

3. What do you think the person in the window is looking at? What does this painting remind you of?

4. Tell about your favorite parts of this painting. Explain why you like them.

Jacob Lawrence. *"In a Free Government, the security of civil rights must be the same as that for religious rights. . . ."* *(the words of James Madison)*, 1976. Opaque watercolor and pencil on paper, mounted on fiberboard, 30 by 22⅛ inches. Gift of the Container Corporation of America. National Museum of American Art, Smithsonian Institution, Washington, D.C./Art Resource, New York. Courtesy of the artist and Francine Seders Gallery, Seattle, Washington.

Unit 2

Cultural Expressions

Earth is home to many cultures. Artists make visual records of these cultures. Their artworks may show landmarks or community leaders. Others show ideas about food, clothing, or shelter that make a culture special. What visual records of your culture would you like to show?

Meet the Artist

Jacob Lawrence. *Self-Portrait,* 1977.

Jacob Lawrence's art tells the history and culture of twentieth-century African Americans. Lawrence began making art with only a few poster paints. He once said, "Limiting yourself . . . forces you to be more inventive." He later created some groups of paintings that tell stories of African American families. Watch for another artwork by Lawrence later in this unit.

Color

Colors, or hues, help artists of every culture express their thoughts and feelings. Point to red and blue on the color wheel on page 53. Where do you see these hues in *Geraniums Before Blue Mountain?*

Auguste Macke. *Geraniums Before Blue Mountain,* date unknown. Oil on canvas, 20½ by 25½ inches. Milwaukee Art Museum. Gift of Mrs. Harry Lynde Bradley.

Color Wheel

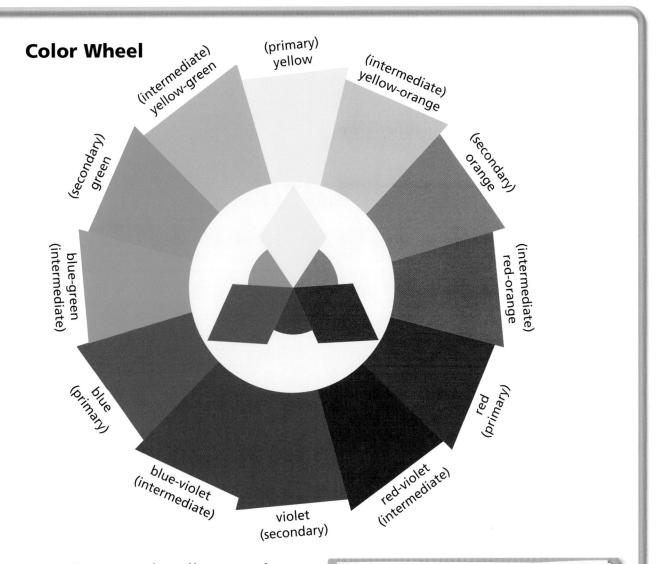

(primary) yellow

(intermediate) yellow-orange

(secondary) orange

(intermediate) red-orange

red (primary)

red-violet (intermediate)

violet (secondary)

blue-violet (intermediate)

blue (primary)

blue-green (intermediate)

(secondary) green

(intermediate) yellow-green

Point to red, yellow, and blue on the color wheel. They are the **primary colors.** If you mix two primary colors, you get a **secondary color.** Find a secondary color on the color wheel. To make an **intermediate color,** mix a primary color and a secondary color. Look again at Macke's painting. What intermediate colors do you see? Choose one. What hues did Macke mix to get that color?

Sketchbook Journal

Use oil pastels to practice mixing colors. Make some secondary and intermediate hues. Blend colors together with a tissue.

Paint a Rainbow

Paint a rainbow of primary, secondary, and intermediate colors. Use primary colors and white as your tools.

1 Mix white paint with blue. Brush it over your paper to show the sky.

 2 Mix paints to make secondary and intermediate colors.

Technique Tip

To make violet, start with some white paint. Add a dab of blue. Then add a dab of red. Mix the paints together.

 3 Use primary, secondary, and intermediate colors to paint a rainbow.

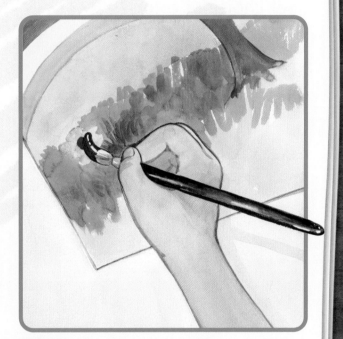 **4** Add details to your painting. Use colors from your rainbow.

Think Like an Artist

What did you learn about mixing colors?
Explain how you made a secondary color.
Describe how you made an intermediate color.

Color Schemes

Frida Kahlo used a **color scheme,** or plan for combining colors, to paint *Long Live Life*. What message do you think the artist wanted to send with her choice of colors?

Frida Kahlo. *Long Live Life (Viva la vida),* 1954. Oil on masonite, 20¼ by 28⅛ inches. Reproduction authorized by the National Institute of Fine Arts and Literature, Mexico City, Mexico.

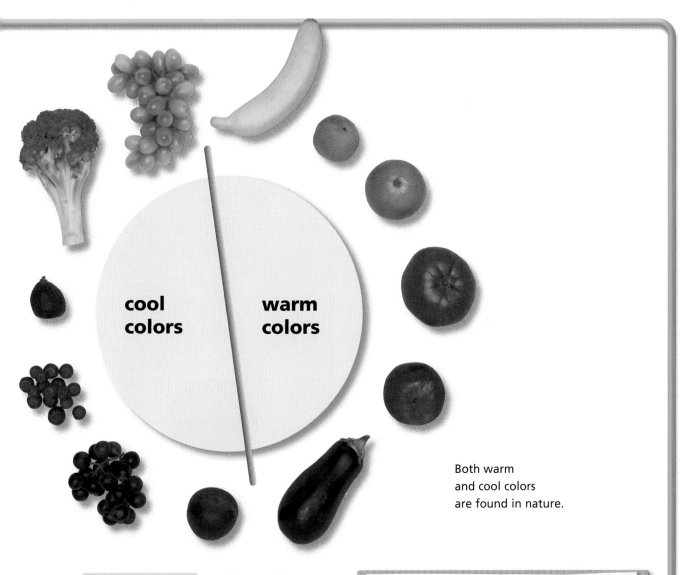

cool colors

warm colors

Both warm and cool colors are found in nature.

Cool colors, such as blues and greens, bring to mind sadness or peacefulness. On the other side of the color wheel are the **warm colors.** Yellows, oranges, and reds may show anger or excitement.

Find green and blue-green on the color wheel. They are **analogous,** or next to each other on the color wheel. **Complementary** colors are opposite each other on the color wheel.

Sketchbook Journal

Cut out colored shapes from magazines. Arrange them into different color schemes. Glue them down and label the groups. Tell about a mood each color group can create.

Draw with Colors

Draw a picture using two complementary colors.
Follow the steps.

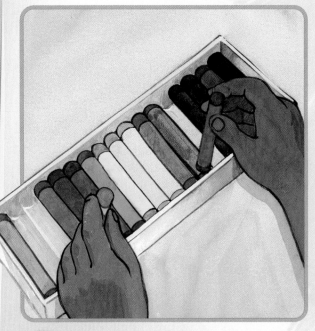

1 Choose a pair of complementary colors in oil pastels.

2 Think about a mood you want to create with the colors.

Technique Tip

Place complementary colors close together to make an area stand out. Separate the colors for a less bold effect in the background.

3 Use your complementary colors to outline areas of the drawing.

4 Add dots, swirls, lines, and other kinds of marks to fill in your drawing.

Think Like an Artist

Do you like the effects of the complementary colors? Explain.

Landmarks and Color

The painting on this page shows different **color values,** or lighter and darker colors. To show color values, artists make tints and shades. Adding a color to white makes a **tint.** To make a **shade,** add black to a color.

Paul Cézanne. *Mont Sainte-Victoire Seen from the Bibemus Quarry,* ca. 1897. Oil on canvas, 25⅓ by 31¼ inches. The Baltimore Museum of Art, Baltimore, MD.

This photograph of Mount Rushmore shows neutral colors.

Name the primary color in this illustration. What would you call the tint and the shade that have been mixed?

Black, white, and gray are **neutral colors.** Some artists use brown as a neutral color, too. Find the neutral colors in the photograph of Mount Rushmore.

The faces of the presidents appear realistic in this landmark. Some artists show fantasy images. These images do not appear real. Which landmarks in your community appear realistic?

Art in My World

Look at landmarks and buildings in your community. What color schemes do they show? Tell why the landmarks are there and what they mean.

Paint a Landmark

Think of a landmark that represents your community.
Now imagine your own version of the same landmark.
Follow these steps to paint both.

1 Divide a sheet of paper in half with a pencil line.

2 Blend color values to show your imaginary landmark.

Technique Tip

To mix gray, add a dab of black to white. To mix brown, start with white. Add dabs of any two complementary colors.

3 Paint your imaginary landmark on one side of the paper.

4 Now paint a realistic picture of your landmark using neutral colors.

Think Like an Artist

What does your landmark tell about your culture?

Community Scenes

Jacob Lawrence. *The Library,* 1960. Tempera on fiberboard, 24 by 29⅞ inches. Smithsonian American Art Museum, Washington, D.C.

Artists may show different parts of their communities in their artworks. Look at this painting of people in the library. Notice the flat shapes and bold colors. Who was the artist?

Richard Estes. *Helene's Florist,* 1971. Oil on canvas, 48 by 72 inches. Toledo Museum of Art, Toledo, OH.

Now look at Richard Estes' flower shop. His details and colors make the sidewalk display look so real you can almost smell the flowers!

In what ways are these paintings alike? How are they different? How did each artist use color to get your attention?

Sketchbook Journal

Draw your own picture of a community scene. Use color to draw a viewer's eye to parts of your artwork. Add details that tell about your community.

Balance

Balance describes the way parts of an artwork are arranged. This principle of design helps make an artwork pleasing. Artists work with three types of balance.

Georgia O'Keeffe. *Evening Star, III,* 1917. Watercolor on paper, 9 by 11⅞ inches. The Museum of Modern Art, New York. Mr. and Mrs. Donald B. Straus Fund. Photograph © 1996. The Museum of Modern Art, New York. © 1997 The Georgia O'Keeffe Foundation/Artists Rights Society (ARS), New York. Photograph © The Museum of Modern Art, New York.

The picture of the butterfly shows **symmetrical balance.** Both sides are about the same. The painting by Georgia O'Keeffe shows **asymmetrical balance.** Each side is not the same, yet the artwork appears balanced and complete.

Now look at the stained-glass window. Its **radial balance** shows the lines, shapes, and colors coming from a center point. Point to an example of radial balance in the painting by O'Keeffe.

Look for examples of symmetry and asymmetry in your community. What type of balance will you show in your artworks?

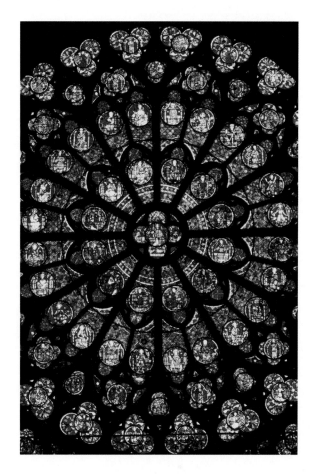

Examples of symmetry are found in art and in nature.

Sketchbook Journal

What type of balance does a horse's face show? Make some drawings. Then add a body and legs. Draw the surroundings. How is the whole drawing balanced?

Design Stained Glass

Artists have used color and the design principle of balance to make beautiful stained-glass windows for centuries. Now you can design one, too.

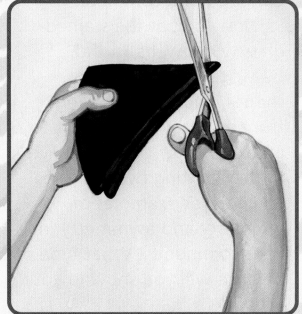

1 Cut a large circle from black construction paper.

2 Fold the circle in half, then in half again, and then once more. Cut off the tip.

Technique Tip

Overlap different colors of tissue paper sheets to add color variety to your window.

3 Snip small shapes along the folds. Open the circle. Spread thin glue over it.

4 Cut tissue paper and arrange it over the holes. Brush thin glue all over.

Think Like an Artist

What kinds of balance does your window show? Are you satisfied with your design? Why or why not?

Pattern

What patterns do you see in these artworks? **Patterns,** or repeated colors, lines, and shapes, add interest to the design. What do you think the title of this quilt means?

Artist unknown, possibly Gertrude Knappenberger. *The Centennial Quilt,* date unknown. Cotton with cotton embroidery, 84 by 74 inches. Collection of the Museum of American Folk Art, NY. Gift of Rhea Goodman, 1979.9.1.

Patterns and symbols can turn functional objects into artworks.

Some artworks have a function, or purpose. Rugs and **quilts** are examples of functional art. Hand-stitched quilts were often made as group projects. Each person might plan and sew one **quilt block,** or square.

Quilts and rugs often include **symbols,** shapes or pictures that represent ideas and values. What might the symbols in these patterns mean?

Sketchbook Journal

Draw a pattern design for an object you can use, such as a dish or a bedspread. Include symbols that hold special meaning for you. Add color to your pattern design.

Studio 5
Design a Quilt

Choose a theme for a class quilt. Then plan your own quilt block of geometric shapes with two classmates.

1 Choose geometric shapes to illustrate your theme. Make sketches of them.

2 Plan a design. Draw the shapes on colored paper.

Technique Tip

Choose simple patterns or symbols that relate to the quilt theme. Avoid images that have too many details.

3 Cut out your shapes. Glue them in place on the quilt block.

4 Add the group blocks to a bulletin-board display of the class quilt.

Think Like an Artist

Describe the symbols on each quilt block. Tell what they mean.

Prints

The artworks on these pages are prints. Both prints show cultural leaders or public figures. To make a **print,** artists apply ink to a surface, or **print block.** Then they press paper onto the print block. Or, they press the print block onto paper.

Max Weber. *Rabbi Reading,* 1919. Woodcut, printed in color, composition, 4³⁄₁₆ by 1¹⁵⁄₁₆ inches. The Museum of Modern Art, New York. Gift of Abby Aldrich Rockefeller. Photograph © 1996. The Museum of Modern Art, New York.

Andy Warhol. *Moonwalk,* 1987. Screenprint, 38 by 38 inches. Courtesy of Ronald Feldman Fine Arts, New York. © 1997 Andy Warhol Foundation for the Visual Arts/Ronald Feldman Fine Arts/ARS, New York. Photograph by D. James Dee.

To make a **relief print,** artists carve a design into a print block. Then they use a **brayer,** a rubber roller, to apply ink to the raised or uncarved surface. Finally, they press the block onto paper.

Read the credit lines for the prints on these two pages. What two cultures are represented? What do you think the prints show you about the beliefs of these cultures?

Sketchbook Journal

What symbols are part of your family or culture? Draw a sketch for a relief print that shows what is important in your culture. Explain the meaning of the symbols to a friend.

Make a Print

Think of a leader or a symbol of leadership in your culture. Follow these steps to make a relief print.

 1 Draw your design on a clean meat tray. This will be your print block.

2 Mix tempera with a bit of dish soap. Roll the paint evenly on your print block.

Technique Tip

Do not put too much paint on the brayer or on the print block. The paint should *not* fill in the lines you carved.

 3 Place a clean sheet of paper on top of your design. Rub it gently with your hands.

4 Slowly pull the print. Let it dry completely.

Think Like an Artist

How does the color you used help show your cultural leader or symbol?

Printmaking

Annemaree Rea is a printmaker. Artists who specialize in making prints may use many different materials and nearly any subject for their artworks. Rea might get an idea for a print from almost anything, even trash! A picture from a children's book may become the subject of one of her prints. Whatever the subject though, the final print is her own work.

Rea uses many printmaking techniques. One is relief printing. The printmaker carves an image into a block using special tools. Then she places paper or fabric over the top and uses a heavy press to transfer the image from the block to the paper or fabric.

Some of Rea's prints become greeting cards. Other prints may hang in art galleries for people to buy. Rea does not try to sell all of her artworks, though. She trades some with other artists whose work she likes.

Rea takes pleasure from the sense of order that comes from making multiple copies. Also, she says, "When you make a print, you're making a little piece of you for the whole world to see—a hundred times!"

Printmaker Annemaree Rea at work

Annemaree Rea.
No Added Hormones,
2003. Linocut.

Annemaree Rea. *Run,* 2002. Collagraph.

Annemaree Rea.
Hide, 2003. Inkjet
study for four-color
lithography.

79

Make Gadget Prints

What kinds of designs can you make with gadgets?
Use gadgets and your imagination to make prints.

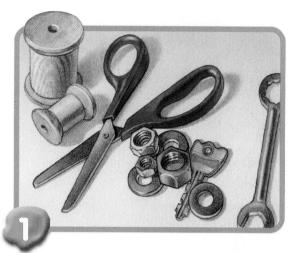

1 Plan a real or imaginary design. Choose some gadgets to use in your print.

2 Dip the gadgets into neon tempera paint and press them onto your paper.

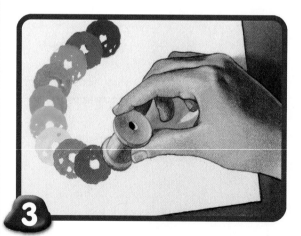

3 Overlap some of the shapes. Create symmetrical or asymmetrical balance.

4 Let it dry. Then use chalk pastels to fill in with a variety of lines and shapes.

Rachel, Age 10. *Flamingo Land.*
Tempera and chalk pastels.

What type of balance did these students show? Do you see any patterns?

Elizabeth, Age 9. *X.* Tempera and chalk pastels.

Share Your Art

1. Identify the gadgets you used in your print.

2. Explain the type of balance your print shows.

Unit Review

Think About Art

Read the art words. Then explain how either picture relates to each term.

primary color   tint   balance
warm and cool colors shade   pattern

Write About Art

What color scheme is used in a place where you spend a lot of time? What message do you think the color scheme sends to anyone entering this place? Write about your special place.

Talk About Art

- Look through your portfolio.
- Choose an artwork that you especially like.
- Tell someone how you made it. Talk about decisions you made about color and balance.
- What might someone learn about your culture from this artwork?

Henri Rousseau. *Tropical Storm with a Tiger (Surprise),* 1891. Oil on canvas, 51⅛ by 31⁹⁄₁₆ inches. Trustees, National Gallery, London.

Put It All Together

1. What color scheme did Rousseau use?

2. What type of balance does this artwork show? Explain.

3. What mood does this painting express?

4. The title suggests that the artist wanted to send the viewer a message about storminess and surprise. Was he successful? Explain.

Louise Nevelson. *Royal Tide I,* 1960. Wood painted gold, 96 by 40 by 8 inches. Collection of Peter and Beverly Lipman.

Unit 3

Expression in Art

Artists express their thoughts and feelings through their work. Some artworks make people laugh or cry. Others make people ask questions. Many artists express themselves by making **forms.** These **three-dimensional** artworks have height, width, and depth. Forms may be delicate necklaces or huge public buildings. What three-dimensional artworks have you seen?

Meet the Artist

At an early age, sculptor Louise Nevelson was asked what she wanted to do when she grew up. "I'm going to be an artist," she replied. Then she added, "No, I'm going to be a sculptor. I don't want color to help me." Indeed, Nevelson's artworks are mostly collections of found objects painted a single color—black, white, or gold.

Decorative and Useful

Artists create **decorative artworks** to add interest and beauty to surroundings. A painting that hangs on a wall is an example. Other artworks may have a function, or purpose, and are known as **functional artworks.** Often, functional art, such as furniture or clothing, is also decorative.

Artist unknown, Bamana culture. *Antelope Headdress,* late 19th–early 20th century. Wood. North Carolina Museum of Art, Raliegh, NC.

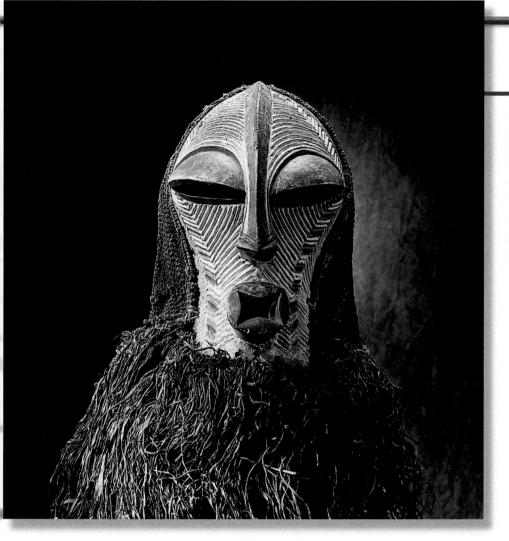

Artist unknown, African. *Kifwebe Mask,* date unknown. Wood fiber, pigments and feathers, 14⅞ by 8⅛ inches. © Royal Museum of Central Africa, Tervuren, Belgium.

In many cultures, people wear **headgear,** or hats. These artworks have different purposes. Some hats may be worn as protection from the weather. Others are worn as ceremonial dress.

Masks, another type of three-dimensional artwork, are often worn during cultural ceremonies. Sometimes masks and headgear are worn together.

Sketchbook Journal

Let the objects on these pages inspire you. Draw yourself wearing an imaginative mask. What headgear might you add to your drawing?

Make a Paper Hat

Design a three-dimensional paper hat to express your mood. Make it decorative, functional, or both.

1 Make a sketch as a design for your hat.

2 Gather lightweight materials as decorations for surface texture.

Technique Tip

Arrange objects, such as bottle caps, buttons, and sequins, as a decorative surface texture for your hat.

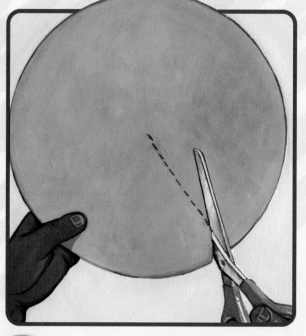

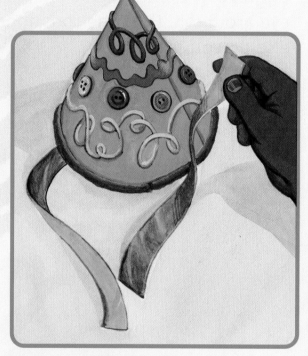

3 Cut out a large circle. Slit to center. Staple into a cone.

4 Glue on the decorations. Wear your hat for a celebration!

Think Like an Artist

How might you use or display your paper hat? Would you describe it as functional, decorative or both? Explain your answer.

Rhythm in Forms

Artists show movement, or **rhythm,** in artworks such as this one. Notice the elements of art that seem to move. Flickering flame shapes on the circle lead the eye around it. Even the toes appear to move. Where else do you see rhythm?

Artist unknown. *Nataraja: Siva as King of Dance.* South India, Chola Period, 11th century. Bronze, height 44½ inches. © The Cleveland Museum of Art, 1996, purchase from the J. H. Wade Fund, 1930.331.

How do the arms in this form suggest movement?

Abastenia St. Leger Eberle. *Roller Skating,* ca. 1906. Bronze, 12¹³⁄₁₆ by 11¼ by 6½ inches. Photograph © 1996 Whitney Museum of American Art, New York. Gift of Gertrude Vanderbilt Whitney. Photograph by Geoffrey Clements.

Artists may choose from a variety of materials, or **media,** to create artworks. Look at the credit lines to see what **medium** each of these artists used. Some types of media are clay, fabric, paint, and charcoal. How do the media in these sculptures help create a sense of rhythm?

Sketchbook Journal

Draw some flames, waves, trees, or other natural forms that show movement. Practice showing visual rhythm in a variety of ways using lines, shapes, and colors.

Create a Foil Sculpture

What kind of movement do you enjoy most? Is it kicking a soccer ball or skateboarding down a hill? Make a form that shows movement.

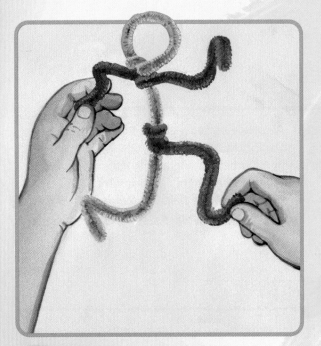

1 Build an armature, or frame, to show a figure in motion.

2 Wrap strips of aluminum foil around the frame of your form.

Technique Tip

Draw a sketch of the motion you want your figure to express or show. Refer to your sketch as you make the armature.

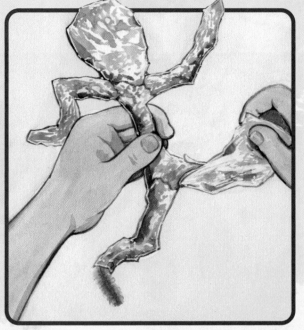

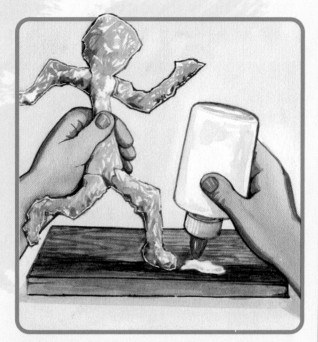

3 Wrap and shape the foil to cover the entire form.

4 Attach the sculpture to a sturdy base of cardboard, wood, or foam.

Think Like an Artist

Have a friend act out the motion shown in your sculpture. Compare the lines of the rhythm with those of your artwork.

Emphasis in Forms

Dale Chihuly wanted one part of his artwork to stand out. He created **emphasis** with color. The bright color draws your eye to the pink flower-like form. This is the artwork's **center of interest.**

Dale Chihuly. *Red Ikebana Flower,* 2001. Blown glass, length 14 inches. Collection of the artist.

Chihuly used color to create emphasis. Other artists might use size, placement, or shape.

Artist unknown, Navajo culture. *Squash Blossom Necklace,* 1910–1925. Silver. Museum of Fine Arts, Houston, TX.

Rings, bracelets, necklaces, and earrings are all common forms of **jewelry.** Often jewelry is made of precious metals and gems. Many items of jewelry are designed with a center of interest. Point to the center of interest in the squash blossom necklace.

Would you say that jewelry is decorative, functional, or both? Explain.

Studio 3

Make a Pendant

Create a foil pendant that shows emphasis. Then make the pendant into a necklace.

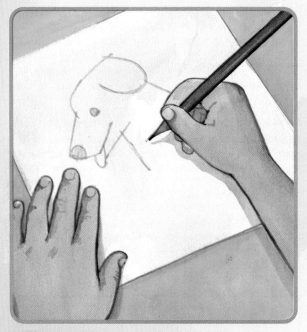

1 Sketch a pendant design that expresses a special interest. Show emphasis.

2 Place the design on top of the copper foil. Go over the lines with a dull pencil.

Technique Tip

Show emphasis by making one area more detailed or bold in color. Make your shape unusual in size.

3 Use tools to create a repeating pattern for the background.

4 Punch a hole in the pendant and string a heavy cord through it.

Think Like an Artist

How did you use lines and shapes to show emphasis?

Forms and Media

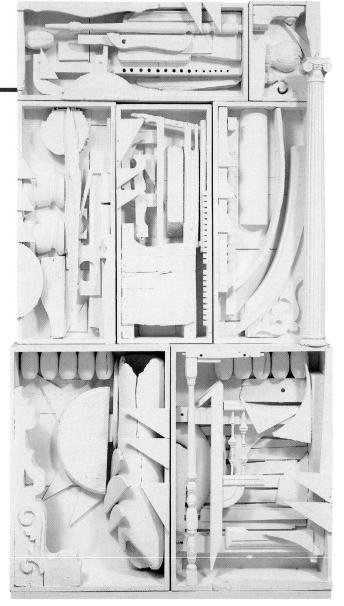

Louise Nevelson. *Dawn's Wedding Chapel I,* 1959. Wood painted white, 90 by 51 by 6 inches. Courtesy of the Estate of Louise Nelson. The Pace Gallery, New York. Photograph by Bill Jacobson.

These two artworks show some of the different choices sculptors make about form, media, shape, and color. These choices help the artists express themselves.

You saw another sculpture by Louise Nevelson on page 84. Both she and sculptor Nancy Graves often used everyday objects in their artworks.

Compare these two artworks. How have the artists' choices of media, color, and shape contributed to the mood of each sculpture? Which one would you prefer to have in your room? Why?

Nancy Graves. *Tarot,* 1984. Bronze with polychrome patina and enamel, 88 by 49 by 20 inches. Courtesy of Knoedler & Company, New York. © 1998 Nancy Graves Foundation/ Licensed by VAGA, New York.

Sketchbook Journal

Sketch a sculpture you would like to create. Express a mood through your sketch. Make notes about the colors and media you would use to make the sculpture.

Pop Art

Do these sculptures make you hungry? Watch out! You could chip a tooth if you took a bite. Read the credit line to discover the medium the artist used. These food forms are made in a style called **Pop Art,** which began in the 1950s.

Claes Oldenburg. *Pastry Case, I,* 1961–1962. Enamel paint on nine plaster sculptures in glass case, 20¾ by 30⅛ by 14¾ inches. The Sidney and Harriet Janis Collection, The Museum of Modern Art, New York.

Pop artists like Claes Oldenberg use everyday objects such as food, soup cans, typewriters, and boxes of steel wool as subjects for their artworks.

David Gilhooly. *Frog Sandwich,* 1990. Ceramic, 2½ by 4½ by 4 inches. Collection of Fenton Fine Arts, Fort Worth, TX. Photograph by David Wharton.

Ceramic artworks like *Frog Sandwich* are made from clay. **Clay** is a soft, moist medium dug from the ground. After the form is shaped, the artist fires it in a kiln, or special oven. After the object cools, the artist paints it with glaze. **Glaze** is a mix of water and minerals that produce different colors. Then the clay object is fired again.

What mood do you think these sculptors tried to create?

Sketchbook Journal

Draw a picture of yourself eating your favorite food. How will you show the color and texture of the food in your drawing? How might you add humor to it?

Studio 4

Make a Pop Art Meal

What favorite food would you like to bring to a meal? Make a sculpture of that food.

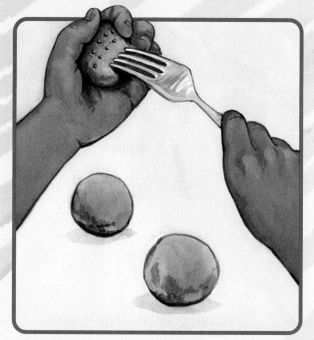

1 Use your fingers or tools to mold a type of food from clay.

2 Add designs to the surface or apply small pieces for details. Let it dry.

Technique Tip

Use kitchen tools and other gadgets to create the texture of your food.

 3 Paint your sculpture with glazes or acrylic paints.

4 Make a table setting with some friends. Present the food you made.

Think Like an Artist

How did you use shapes, forms, textures, and colors to make your Pop Art food look almost real?

Design in Architecture

The art of designing buildings is called **architecture.** Artists who design buildings are called **architects.** They make plans for homes, schools, stores, museums, and other structures. As they plan, architects use forms such as cubes, cylinders, pyramids, and cones. These forms give height, width, and depth to the structures.

Exterior of the Pantheon, Rome, Italy.

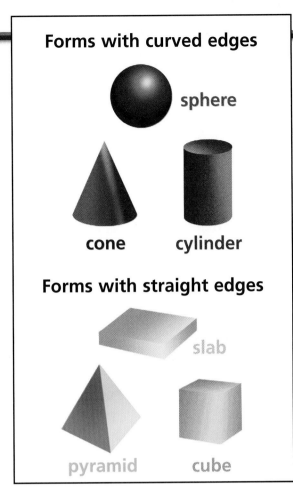

Forms with curved edges

sphere

cone   cylinder

Forms with straight edges

slab

pyramid   cube

Where do you see these forms in the Pantheon?

The Pantheon has influenced the design of many other buildings around the world.

An architect asks many questions to plan a building. How will the building be used? Where will it be located? Next, the architect makes a floor plan, or map, of the rooms. Often the architect will make a three-dimensional **model** to show how the structure will look. Finally, the architect makes a drawing, or blueprint. Builders use this drawing to construct the building.

Art in My World

Look around your community. What forms are included in the design of the public buildings? Find out when the buildings were built. Who designed them?

105

Make a Model

Work with a group to design a model of an art center for the future. Plan together how people might use different areas of the art center.

1 Get some ideas from buildings of the past.

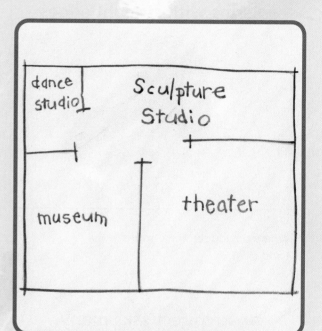

2 Make a floor plan. Then decide what shape the outside will take.

Technique Tip

Add pencil or marker details before you put the building parts together. It is easier to add fine details when the pieces are lying flat.

3 Create forms from heavy paper or found objects. Glue or tape the forms together.

4 Place the museum model on a base. Add details to the outdoor spaces.

Think Like an Artist

Does your three-dimensional model look like your two-dimensional sketches or floor plan? How are they alike and different?

Sculpture and the Land

Some artists design structures for **outdoor spaces.** These may be large sculptures, such as the one below, made of soft materials that wash away. Other outdoor structures may be **monuments** that are built in memory of people or events.

Andy Goldsworthy. *Sand Brought to an Edge to Catch the Light,* August, 1991. Shore of Lake Michigan. © Andy Goldsworthy. Photograph courtesy of the artist.

Maya Ying Lin. *Vietnam Veterans Memorial,* 1981. Black granite monument.

Names of Americans who died in the Vietnam War are carved on the monument.

Artist Andy Goldsworthy uses natural materials for his outdoor sculptures. The materials come from the area where he builds the sculpture. Some of his sculptures last only a few hours.

Maya Ying Lin designed the Vietnam Veterans Memorial. It seems a natural part of the land around it. The black granite walls resemble a scar in the earth. What do you think the artist was saying?

Art in My World

Look around for natural materials that you could use in an outdoor structure. Sketch what the structure might look like. What ideas will your structure convey?

109

Design a Monument

Brainstorm about some historic people and events.
Then choose one as the subject of a monument.

1 Draw some designs that show your subject. Choose one.

2 Use paper or foam forms for the monument and its base.

Technique Tip

Score foam by running the sharp edge of scissors along a line you have drawn on the foam. Bend the foam on the line to break it.

3 Attach everyday objects. Then attach your monument to a base. Add details.

4 Write words for a plaque, or sign.

Think Like an Artist

Discuss how your monument expresses the importance of the person or event.

Pottery

Les Orenstein is a grown-up, but he likes to play with clay. Of course, Orenstein works with clay for a living so it is all in a day's work. As a ceramist, Orenstein gets ideas from other potters. Some lived thousands of years ago; others are his friends today. Orenstein also gets ideas for his own artworks by observing his family and the world around him.

The artist tries to keep the principles of design in mind as he makes a pot or other ceramic artwork. Still, during the firing process, surprises occur. According to Orenstein, "There are different things that make a pot special—the color, the shape, the surface. You don't have control over all of them."

Orenstein finds satisfaction in keeping up a tradition that goes back thousands of years. He also likes the way his work combines so many elements of nature—earth, fire, and water.

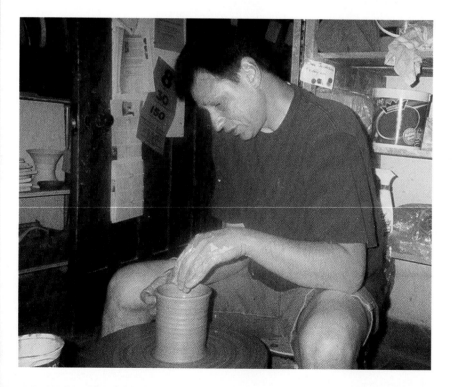

Les Orenstein working at a potter's wheel in his studio

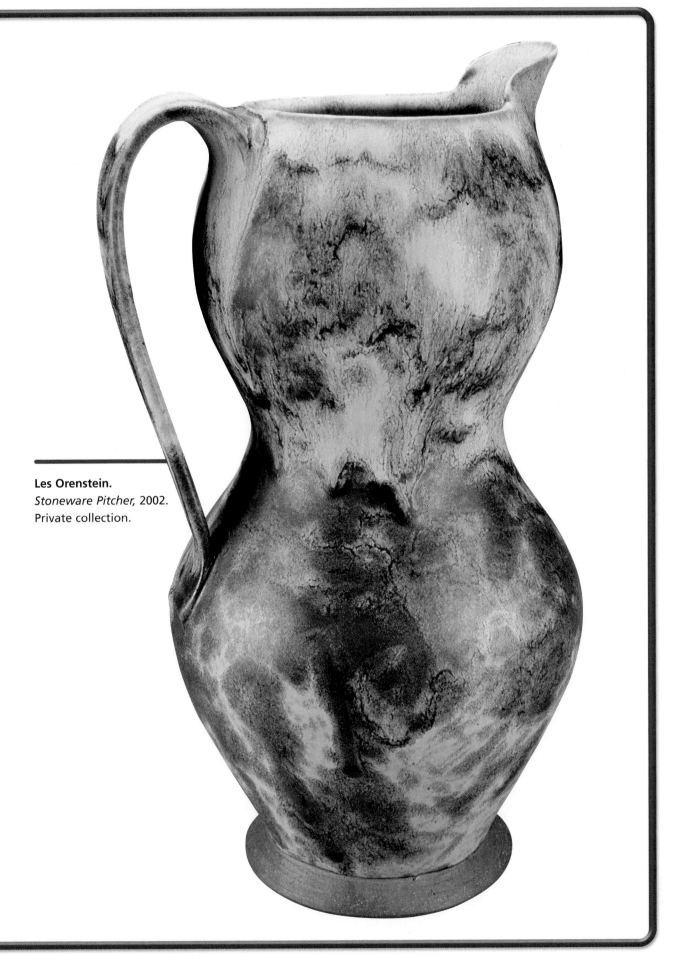

Les Orenstein.
Stoneware Pitcher, 2002.
Private collection.

Make a Miniature Mask

Make a miniature mask to decorate your wall. Will your mask resemble a person, an animal, or a fantasy character?

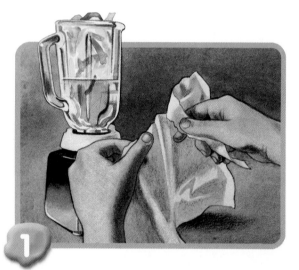

1 Shred newsprint and tissue paper. Your teacher will blend with water.

2 Scoop the pulp onto a piece of screen and gently blot it with paper towels.

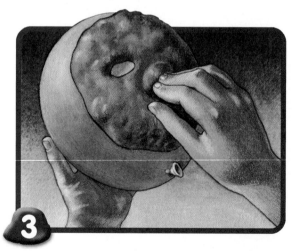

3 Place the damp pulp on a balloon. Add layers to build up features from the surface. Let it dry.

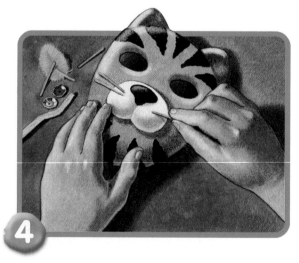

4 Remove the balloon. Paint your mask. Add decorative objects.

Emily, Age 9. *Mask of the Kiwi People.* Newsprint and tissue paper.

Gage, Age 9. *Mask of the Square Face.* Newsprint and tissue paper.

These masks were designed by other fourth-graders. How might they be used?

Share Your Art

1. Compare molding paper with molding clay.

2. What is successful about your miniature mask? Explain.

Think About Art

Read the art words. Then explain how one or more of the pictures relates to each term.

three-dimensional functional art

center of interest monument

decorative art rhythm

Write About Art

Write about how an artist's choice of form and media can help express an idea or feeling. Use artwork from this unit to explain your ideas.

Talk About Art

- Look through your portfolio.
- Choose the artwork that you think is most rhythmic or interesting in some way.
- Tell a classmate what you like about it.
- Use words such as *media, rhythm,* and *emphasis.*

Put It All Together

1. *Cadillac Ranch* is a monument in a large outdoor space in Texas. Describe the lines, shapes, and forms.

2. How are the forms alike? What effect does the unusual position of the cars create?

3. In what way is the sculpture's style similar to Pop Art? Do you think this sculpture is meant to be humorous or serious? Why?

4. If you could ask the artists of this sculpture a question, what would it be?

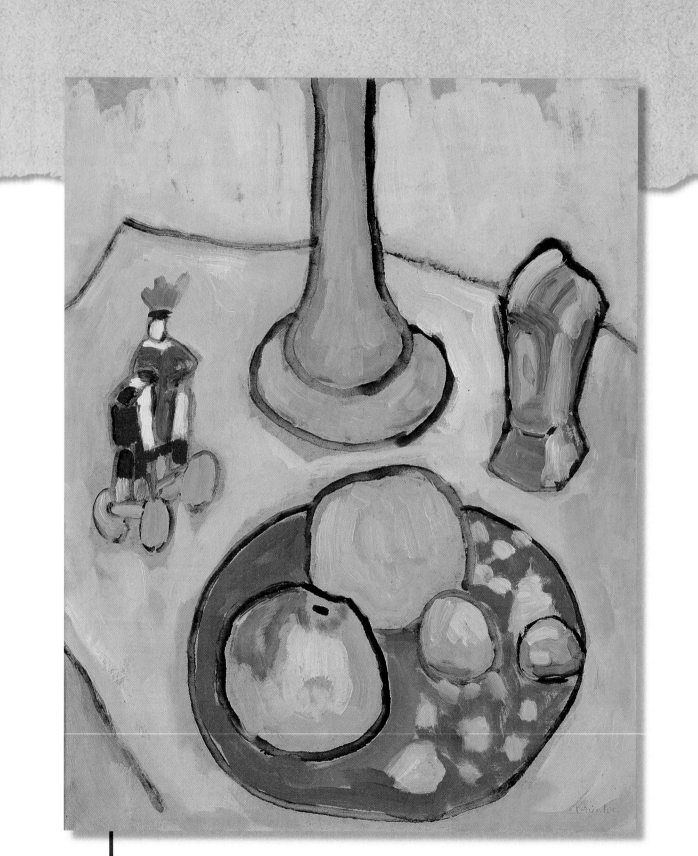

Gabriele Münter. *Yellow Still Life,* 1909. Oil on cardboard, 16½ by 13 inches. Millwaukee Art Museum, gift of Mrs. Lynde Bradley, M1975.1556. Photo by Larry Saunders.

Creative Expression

Artists express their ideas, thoughts, and feelings through their artworks. Some artists express themselves by exploring a variety of media. Others use a single medium and may experiment with different subjects. How do *you* express yourself through art?

Meet the Artist

Portraits of Gabriele Münter show the artist as a sweet, dainty woman. In fact, this artist was an important figure in the world of art. She played a large role in the rise of an art movement in Germany in the early twentieth century. Watch for another artwork by Münter later in this unit.

Wassily Kandinsky. *Lady (Portrait of Gabriele Münter),* ca. 1910.

Collage

When Henri Matisse's eyesight began to fail, he put down his paintbrush. Then he picked up his scissors. He used them to create colorful **collages,** works made of torn or cut paper, fabric, or other materials.

Henri Matisse. *The Snail,* 1953. Gouache on cut-and-pasted paper, 112¾ by 113 inches. The Tate Gallery, London.

Pablo Picasso. *Violin and Sheet Music,* 1912. Gouache and paper collage, 30⅔ by 24¾ inches. Musée Picasso, Paris.

Matisse's collage is not a **realistic** view of a snail. It does not look real. Still, it does have a recognizable subject. Look for the spiral snail shape. An artwork that does not have a realistic subject is **abstract.**

Like Matisse, Picasso made collages. This **still life** shows objects that cannot move on their own. Each artwork has a **theme,** or artist's message about the subject.

Research

Pablo Picasso created some of the first collages and helped develop an art style known as Cubism. Research other art styles that show artists' expressions.

Studio 1

Make a Still-Life Collage

Many artists create still-life images in the medium of collage.

1 Choose a subject and a theme for your collage.

2 Collect the shapes, textures, and colors you will use.

Technique Tip

As you prepare the paper bits for your collage, cut some with scissors. Tear others with your fingers.

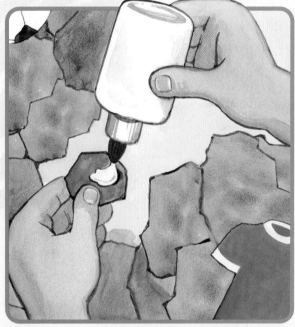

3 Prepare bits of paper. Arrange shapes and paper bits into a pleasing design.

4 Fill in the background with paper bits.

Think Like an Artist

Are you satisfied with your still-life collage?
What might you do differently?

Unity and Variety

The similar lines, shapes, and colors of this map give it **unity.** These elements of art work together to create a feeling that the artwork is complete. However, all the lines, shapes, and colors are not exactly alike. In this way, the combination of elements provides **variety.**

Jasper Johns. *Map,* 1961. Oil on canvas, 78 by 128 inches. Museum of Modern Art, New York.
©2003 Jasper Johns/Licensed by VAGA, New York, NY.

Nam June Paik. *Space Kid,* 1991. Video sculpture, 49 by 58 by 11 inches. Courtesy Carl Solway Gallery, Cincinnati, OH. Photo by Chris Gomien.

Nam June Paik's video sculpture is very different from Jasper Johns's painting. Yet both show unity and variety.

Think about Nam June Paik's use of line, shape, and color. How did he create unity? Do you see variety in the video sculpture? Tell what elements of art the artist used to create variety.

Sketchbook Journal

Design an artwork that could be titled either *Map 2* or *Space Kid 2*. Think of a medium that would suit your idea. Draw a plan that shows unity and variety.

Draw with Oil Pastels

Maps, telephone books, and bus schedules all share a theme of organization. Choose a familiar system that creates order as a subject for an oil pastel drawing.

1 With an oil pastel, draw an object or system that creates order.

2 Lightly draw only a few details to show how the system works.

Technique Tip

If you need to make a change, scrape oil pastel off the paper with a plastic knife, or draw over the area with another color.

 Color your drawing using oil pastels. Add words with markers.

 Blend some colors. Then add a few more details.

Think Like an Artist

How does your artwork show unity and variety?
Explain.

Photography

Photography is the process of capturing images on film, videotape, or another medium. You often see **still photography** when you read a newspaper or open a textbook. Have you seen a photograph of your family? Explain.

Annie Leibovitz. *Louise Bourgeois, Sculptor,* 1999. Black and white photograph. © Annie Leibovitz-Contact Press Images.

Imogen Cunningham. *My Father at Ninety,* 1936. Photograph, 9½ by 7½ inches. Portland Museum of Art, Portland, OR. Copyright 1970 Imogen Cunningham Trust.

Photographers may use their work to record history, tell a story, or help viewers think about a subject in a new way. Many photographers make black-and-white photographs. Look at the values in the photographs on these pages. The differences in light and dark areas add interest. The neutral colors of black, gray, white, and sometimes brown help guide your eye.

How are these two photographs alike? How are they different from color photographs you have seen?

Art in My World

Find a black-and-white photograph in a newspaper, magazine, or other source. How does the photograph express the photographer's point of view toward or feelings about the subject? Write about it.

Make a Photograph

Use black-and-white photography to express a mood or idea or just to show interesting shadows and textures.

 1 Choose an area or a detail to photograph with black-and-white film.

2 Using crayons or charcoal, draw a plan for your black-and-white photograph.

Technique Tip

To take a photograph, frame the scene through the viewfinder. Keep the camera steady by holding your elbows against your body.

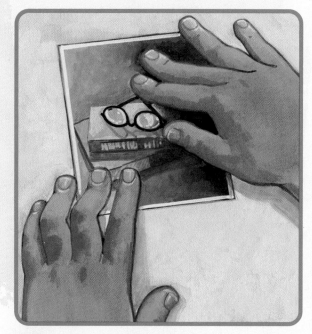

 3 Look through the camera lens. Focus on the subject. Take the photograph.

4 After your photograph is developed, mount it on poster board. Give it a title.

Think Like an Artist

In what way is your photograph different from the drawing you planned? Explain.

Outdoor Scenes

Gabriele Münter. *Cliff Portion of Bornholm*, 1919. Oil on canvas, 14 by 21 inches. Gabriele Münter and Johannes Eichner-Stiftung, Munich, Germany.

One way to discover artists' styles is to compare their artworks. Both paintings here show outdoor scenes. The credit lines offer some information. What other clues tell you they were painted by different artists?

Georgia O'Keeffe. *Grey Hills,* 1941. Oil on canvas, 20 by 30 inches. Indianapolis Museum of Art, Gift of Mr. and Mrs. James W. Fesler.

Each artwork shows a mood. How would you describe the mood of the cliff scene on page 132? Now look at the desert hills shown above. They express a different mood. Notice the contrast of light and dark values on the hills. Does this contrast suggest a humorous or a serious mood? How does the painting make you feel?

Sketchbook Journal

Draw an outdoor scene. Use contrast to help show a mood. Your scene could include people, buildings, and natural objects. How will you express your own style?

Moving Pictures

Do you like to watch cartoons? They are a form of **animation,** a process of putting drawings or photographs together in a way that suggests motion. Each still picture appears in a frame. Each frame shows a picture that is slightly different from the one before it. Thousands of frames are joined to make a reel of film. A light shines through the moving film to display a **motion picture.**

Each motion picture frame is like a page in a flipbook.

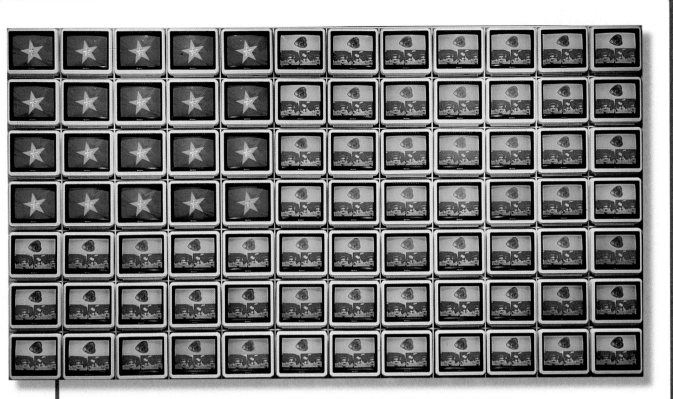

Nam June Paik. *Video Flag Z,* 1985. Television sets, videocassette players, videotapes, plexiglass modular cabinet, 74½ by 138¾ by 18 inches. Los Angeles County Museum of Art. Copyright © 1996 Museum Associates, Los Angeles County Museum of Art. Gift of the Art Museum Council.

Video art is another type of picture that moves. It uses television pictures as an art form. Artist Nam June Paik is a leader in this medium. He mixes video with other media, such as music and still photography.

What are some other ideas that you think would make interesting subjects for a work of video art?

Art Fact

The first television was demonstrated in London in 1926. People in the United States did not begin to buy television sets until almost twenty years later.

135

Make a Zoetrope

Make your own moving pictures with this zoetrope.

 1 Cut an 8-inch circle and a 24-by-3-inch strip from poster board.

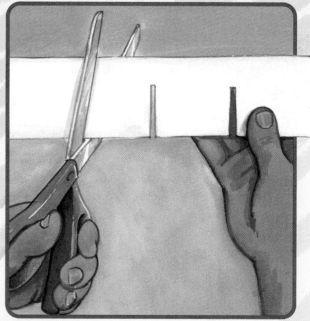

2 Mark every 2 inches on the long edge of the strip. Cut a 1-inch slot on each mark.

Technique Tip

Show only slight changes from one picture to the next. Do not use too much detail in your drawings.

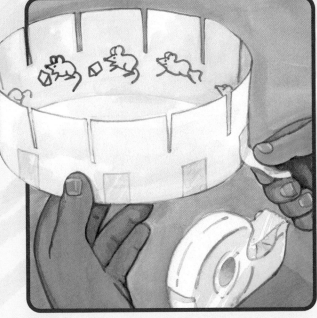

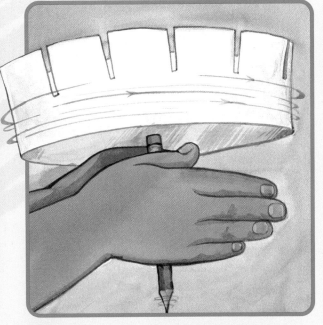

3 Make drawings between each slot. Attach the strip to the base.

4 Thumbtack the base to a pencil eraser. Spin the pencil between your hands.

Think Like an Artist

Does your zoetrope show the motion you hoped for? What changes would you make to improve it?

Artists See Places

Artist Paul Gauguin left Europe to live on a South Pacific island. Many of his artworks show **landscapes,** or outdoor scenes, from the island of Tahiti.

Paul Gauguin. *Tahitian Landscape,* 1891. Oil on canvas, 26¾ by 36½ inches. The Julius C. Eliel Memorial Fund. The Minneapolis Institute of Arts.

Helen Frankenthaler.
Interior Landscape, 1964.
Acrylic on canvas, 104⅞
by 92⅝ inches. San
Francisco Museum of
Modern Art. Gift of the
Women's Board.

You can tell that Gauguin's colorful painting of Tahiti is a landscape even though it does not look just as it would in real life. The artwork is done in an **Expressionist** style. Painters of this movement do not try to paint realistically. Instead, they express their ideas or feelings through the use of bold colors and shapes. Frankenthaler's painting is also of the Expressionist style. Her artwork is abstract. The title of an abstract artwork may help you understand the artist's ideas.

What ideas or feelings do you think are expressed in these paintings? How do the colors and styles of the paintings create or add to that message?

Sketchbook Journal

Have you ever dreamed about a place that didn't seem real? Draw an abstract landscape from memory.

Draw a Landscape

Recall a landscape that made an impression on you, or think of a real or imaginary scene you would like to visit.

1 Think of a realistic or abstract landscape. Draw it with a colored pencil.

2 Add details to show the season, time of day, and weather.

Technique Tip

Observe an outdoor scene to notice how sunlight affects colors and shadows at different times of the day.

 Think about the colors and details that will help you express your thoughts.

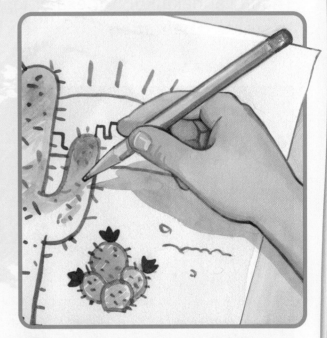 **Color in your landscape, adding the effects of sunlight or moonlight.**

Think Like an Artist

Ask a friend to try to identify the style and mood of your finished landscape.

Technology as Expression

Name some kinds of **technology,** or ways that you use tools and machines. Some artists rely on technology to help them express their thoughts and feelings. Thana Lauhakaikul, for example, used electronic media to create *Celebration.*

Thana Lauhakaikul. *Celebration,* 1983–1985. Mixed-media installation with projected light and sound, 3 by 16 by 25 feet. Photograph courtesy of Chronicle Books.

Ben Livingston. *Neon Mural #1,* 1987. Neon, computer-animated story, 14 by 40 feet. © Ben Livingston. Photograph © Carrington Weems.

Celebration, a **mixed-media** installation, uses more than one medium, including sound and projected light. An **installation** is an artwork that is exhibited for a short time. Then the materials are taken apart and may be moved to another location for exhibition.

Ben Livingston uses technology as his paintbrush. He works with neon and other gases sealed in glass tubes that are bent to make different shapes. *Neon Mural #1* is fourteen feet wide. Where might it fit in your school?

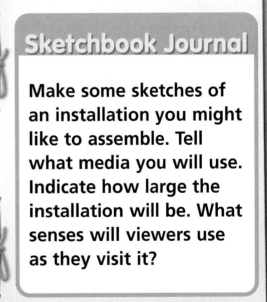

Sketchbook Journal

Make some sketches of an installation you might like to assemble. Tell what media you will use. Indicate how large the installation will be. What senses will viewers use as they visit it?

Create an Installation

Work with other artists—your classmates—to create an installation. Include technology as one of several media in your installation.

 Brainstorm and collect materials and other artworks.

2 **Look over your materials and choose a theme for your installation.**

Technique Tip

Try to add some form of light or sound, such as popular music, that will draw in your viewers.

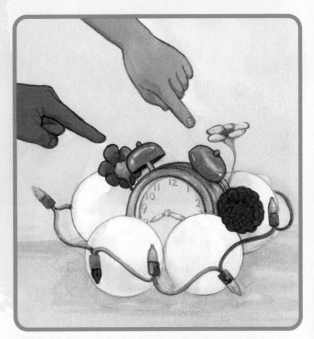

3 Assemble the materials of your installation in an interesting way.

4 Present your installation. Encourage viewers to look closely and ask questions.

Think Like an Artist

What reaction did you hope your installation would produce? Were you successful? Explain.

Photojournalism

Photojournalist Ralph Barrera is always in search of an interesting subject to photograph.

Photojournalist Ralph Barrera might start his day in the newspaper office picking up his assignment. Then he heads out in search of a great shot for a news story. Later, he might work with a photo editor.

Barrera went to college to study engineering. Soon, though, he followed his heart and switched to journalism.

Technology is an important part of Barrera's job. Sometimes he travels with only a laptop computer, camera gear, and a cellular telephone. He uses the laptop and cellular telephone to transmit photographs back to the office. That way the pictures can appear in the newspaper the next day.

What makes a good photograph? Barrera believes it's all about the subject.

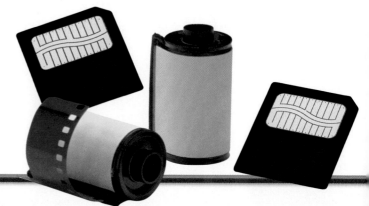

"… Pictures that make you laugh or cry, or keep your interest, … or remind you of someone" are the best. Barrera shows passion about being a photojournalist. "People have been taking pictures for over a hundred years," he says. "I'm just glad I get to take some tomorrow."

Ralph Barrera. *Central Texas Tornado,* 1997. Digital photograph.
© Austin American-Statesman, 1997.

Portfolio Project

Make Abstract Art

Many artists rework themes and subjects to explore different styles. Now it is your turn to change a realistic still life into an abstract artwork.

1 Start by drawing a realistic still life of objects you collect.

2 On heavy paper, draw the still life in a new way. Use geometric forms in an abstract design.

3 Cut materials for your collage. Match the shapes in your abstract drawing.

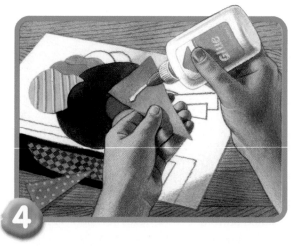

4 Glue materials in place to finish your collage.

Brittany, Age 9. *Glass Fruit.* Collage.

Langley, Age 9. *Raccoon.* Collage.

How do these artworks by other fourth-graders show unity and variety?

Share Your Art

1. What were the subject and theme of your first drawing?

2. Describe the decisions you made as you turned the realistic still life into an abstract artwork. What elements did you use to show unity and variety?

Think About Art

Read the art words. Then use the photographs to find an example for each word.

still life	photography	theme
unity	variety	landscape

Write About Art

You used a variety of media for the artworks in this unit. Name one artwork and write about the process you used to make something.

Talk About Art

- Look through your portfolio.
- Choose an artwork that is one of your best.
- Tell a friend what you tried to show in it.
- Describe unity and variety as they appear in your artwork.

Dorothea Lange. *Migrant Mother, Nipomo, California,* 1936. Black-and-white photograph. © The Dorothea Lange Collection, The Oakland Museum of California, The City of Oakland. Gift of Paul S. Taylor.

Put It All Together

1. Describe the subject and details of this photograph.

2. How do value and contrast help you see that this photograph was taken on a rainy day?

3. The photograph was taken during the Great Depression in a camp of migrant workers. What do you think the photographer was trying to say?

4. Where might you hang this artwork? Explain.

Red Grooms. (Detail) *Ruckus Rodeo,* 1975–1976. Sculpture wire, celastic, acrylic, and burlap, 174 by 606 by 294 inches. Collection of the Modern Art Museum of Fort Worth, Fort Worth, TX.

Unit 5

Art, Old and New

Clothing styles and car designs change from year to year. In fact, many parts of a culture change over time. Art styles, media, and techniques may change too, even as artists borrow from the past. How do you think this large artwork by Red Grooms draws on the past?

Meet the Artist

Artist Red Grooms is known for what he calls his "sculpto-pictoramas." He mixes media in different ways. His scenes are often cartoonlike.

Charles Rogers Grooms was born in Nashville, Tennessee. His nickname, Red, reflects the color of his hair. Look for another artwork by Grooms later in this unit.

Red Grooms. *Self-Portrait as a Bus Driver,* 1998.

Glass

   Some art forms are brand new. Glassmaking, however, has been around for thousands of years. You may think of glass as a material for useful objects, such as windows, light bulbs, or drinking glasses. Glass is also a medium for decorative objects.

Artist unknown, Roman Empire (probably Italy). *Ribbon Glass Cup,* ca. first century A.D. Translucent blue, colorless, green glasses; preformed canes fused, sagged over a mold, and firepolished, 1⅞ by 3½ inches. The Corning Museum of Glass, Corning, NY.

What elements of art show rhythm in this cup?

Glass art uses glass as a medium for decorative or functional artworks. Dale Chihuly is a glass artist whose studio is in Seattle, Washington. He studied glassblowing in Venice, Italy, where the art form has a long **tradition.** The artwork shown here contains nine hundred eighty separate parts of blown glass. The colors were inspired by confetti Chihuly saw in a spring fiesta, or party.

To make glass art, Chihuly first designs the artwork. Then he, or sometimes his team, blows the hot glass and assembles the parts. Compare Chihuly's glass art with the Roman cup. Notice the rhythm shown in each artwork. What mood does each one convey?

Dale Chihuly. *San Antonio Public Library Fiesta Tower,* 2003. Hand-blown glass over steel armature, approximately 21 by 10 feet. San Antonio, TX.

Sketchbook Journal

Use markers to make a sketch of a glass sculpture you might create. Show rhythm. Where would you display your sculpture?

Studio 1

Build a Model

Sculptors often make models before building a sculpture. Make a model for a glass artwork you might want to build.

1 Build an armature of three-dimensional objects.

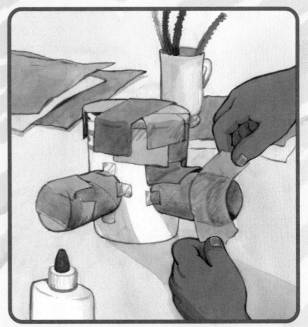

2 Cover the armature with torn strips of tissue paper.

Technique Tip

To create spiral forms, wrap pipe cleaners around a pen or pencil.

3 Use colored markers to add designs.

4 Use pipe cleaners to add interesting lines and forms.

Think Like an Artist

Look at your model from different viewpoints. How does each view change your thinking about the model?

Weaving

Weaving is an ancient art. Navajo women in the southwestern United States have woven beautiful, useful blankets for hundreds of years. This **eye-dazzler blanket** has a colorful design made with dyed wool. The earliest Navajo weavers used mostly undyed wool in natural tones.

Artist unknown, Navajo culture. *Eye-dazzler Blanket,* 1975. Cotton warp, 40¼ by 60¾ inches. School of American Research, Santa Fe, NM. Catalog no. SAR1989-7-352.

In what ways do Navajo artists design and create their weavings?

Traditional weavers use a **loom,** a tool or frame that holds fibers as a weaver works with them. The fibers that stretch vertically on the loom, above, are called the **warp.** The fibers woven from side to side, under and over the warp, are the **weft.**

Today, some weavers plan their designs on computer. They adjust line and color with the help of software. In this way, the artists create one artwork with two media.

Sketchbook Journal

Use colored pencils to draw a design for an eye-dazzler weaving. You may wish to draw a second design on a computer. How would your design show traditional patterns?

Make a Circle Weaving

Create a mixed-media weaving in a circular form. Use paper for the warp and a collection of objects with interesting textures and colors for the weft.

1 Draw and cut out a large circle. Fold it in half.

2 Cut lines from the fold to about an inch from the edge.

Technique Tip

Wrap a small piece of masking tape around the tip of the materials you weave.

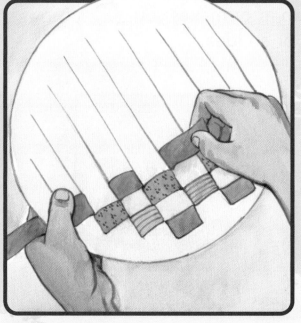

3 Weave the strips over and under. On the next row, go under and over.

4 Trim, then glue the ends of the strips on the edges of the weaving.

Think Like an Artist

Did you use a regular or an irregular pattern in the materials you added for the weft? How would a different pattern change your design?

Cartoons

An artist in the 1400s would have said that a cartoon was a drawing made before creating a final painting or a tapestry, a large woven picture. Today, the word has a different meaning. A **cartoon** is a drawing or animation that pokes fun at or makes you think in a new way about a person or an idea.

PEANUTS, June 24, 2003. PEANUTS reprinted by permission of United Feature Syndicate, Inc.

In what ways does Garfield look like a real cat? Which of his features are *not* realistic?

Cartoons became popular in newspapers in the late 1800s. They were meant for adults and they usually poked fun at politicians.

Today, political cartoons appear on editorial pages of most newspapers. You can also find cartoons, or comic strips, in the funny pages of the newspaper. What are your favorite comic strips and characters? What do you like about them?

Art in My World

Look in a newspaper for a comic strip that appeals to you. Study it to see how the artist uses line and shading and shows motion. Keep checking the strip to watch for new techniques.

Draw a Cartoon

Does a career as a cartoonist seem like fun? Create your own cartoon!

1 Create a cartoon character. Give it unusual features.

2 Draw a plan for the action in three or four frames.

Technique Tip

Give your character a facial feature that will make the character recognizable as well as easy to redraw.

3 Turn your plan into drawings.

4 Write dialogue in speech balloons. Add details to the drawings.

Think Like an Artist

Does your character's appearance match his or her personality? What changes would you make for a better match and more humor?

Passengers

Red Grooms. *Subway (detail from Ruckus Manhattan),* 1976. Mixed media, 108 by 223 by 446 inches. © 1997 Red Grooms/Artists Rights Society (ARS), NY. Photograph courtesy Marlborough Gallery, New York.

Artist Red Grooms observed the subway, or underground train, in New York City as a subject for this artwork. The three-dimensional scene shown here is part of a large multimedia installation.

Frida Kahlo. *The Bus,* 1929. Oil on canvas, 10¼ by 22 inches. Collection of Dolores Olmedo, Mexico City, Mexico.

Frida Kahlo lived and painted in Mexico and the United States. Some viewers think her work has a dreamlike quality, but Kahlo said, "I never painted dreams. I painted my own reality."

Compare the style of *The Bus* with that of *Subway.* How are the subjects and media of these artworks similar and different? How can you tell that the artworks show different places?

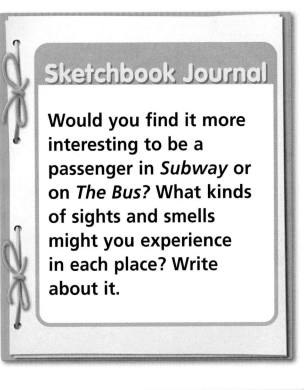

Sketchbook Journal

Would you find it more interesting to be a passenger in *Subway* or on *The Bus?* What kinds of sights and smells might you experience in each place? Write about it.

Industrial Design

Have you ever noticed that many functional objects are beautiful and interesting? Cars, bicycles, appliances, and other machines are examples of **industrial design.** They have a purpose but may also be pleasing to see and use.

Chava Hernandez. *Lowrider Bike,* ca. 1994. Modified Schwinn Sting-Ray bicycle. Photograph © Eric Sander.

Stefano Pirovano.
Pirovano Watch (Calumet 1000 Series), 2000. Urethane, diameter 1½ inches. Museum of Modern Art Design Store, New York. Distributed and marketed by Seiko Instruments (SII), Austin, USA, and Alessi s.p.a., Crusinallo, Italy.

Industrial designers ask themselves many questions as they plan a new design. They must consider an object's purpose as well as how to make it attractive, affordable, and easy to use.

Take a close look at the bicycle and the watch. How do you think the designers answered the following questions: Who will use this object? What kind of design would this person like? What features are important to this user?

Sketchbook Journal

Draw a picture of a brand new design for a bicycle that you would like to ride. Include features that make it attractive or comfortable to use. How would you feel riding this bicycle?

Design with Wire

Industrial design reflects the time in which objects are created. Design a bicycle from the past, present, or future and build it from colored wire.

 1 Draw a design for your bicycle.

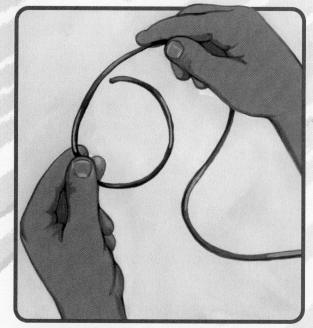

2 Bend and twist the wire for each part of the bicycle.

Technique Tip

When you snip off pieces of wire, hold the wire away from your own and other people's eyes.

3 Connect separate bicycle parts with more wire.

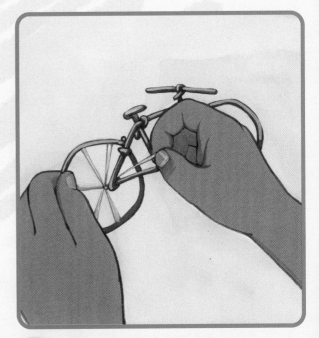

4 Wind and weave more wire to add details to your design.

Think Like an Artist

Describe the kind of person who would enjoy owning the bicycle you designed.

Portraits and Proportion

Long before cameras were invented, artists created portraits. **Portraits** show people or animals as their subjects.

Andy Warhol. *Marilyn,* 1964. Synthetic polymer paint and silkscreen ink on canvas, 40 by 40 inches.

Rembrandt van Rijn. *Self-Portrait,* 1659. Oil on canvas, 33 by 26 inches. Andrew W. Mellon Collection. © 1996 Board of Trustees, National Gallery of Art, Washington, D.C. Photograph by Richard Carafelli.

The portraits on these two pages are from different centuries. How can you tell which one is old and which one is new?

Some artists use themselves as the subjects of their artworks. A **self-portrait** shows an image of the artist.

The **proportions** of a face show how facial features relate to each other in terms of size and placement. For example, notice how the eyes in many portraits fall midway between the top of the head and the chin.

Research

Find a portrait by one of these painters: Diego Velázquez, Mary Cassatt, or Alice Neel. Who is the subject? What can you tell about that person?

Draw a Self-Portrait

Have you ever looked closely at the proportions of your face in a mirror? Studying facial features helps artists draw self-portraits.

 1 Look at your face in a mirror. Notice the size and position of your features.

2 Fold a piece of paper into eight sections.

Technique Tip

Use the side of your pencil point for shading. You can also blend the shadows with a tissue.

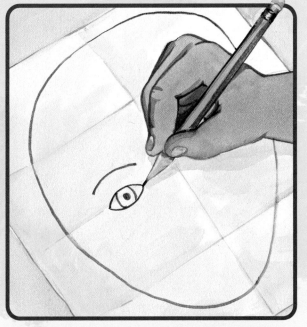

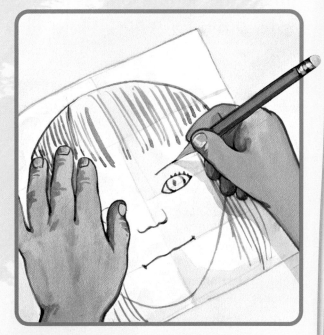

3 Draw your face using the grid as a guide. Look in the mirror as necessary.

4 Place your other features, using the grid to help.

Think Like an Artist

How is your self-portrait likely to be different from a portrait of you painted by someone else?

The Human Form

Throughout history, artists have created artworks showing the entire human form. Portrait painters often show subjects in a realistic **pose,** or position, to make the people look as lifelike as possible. A person who poses for a portrait is called a **model.**

Thomas Gainsborough. *Jonathan Buttall: The Blue Boy,* ca. 1770. Oil on canvas, 70⅝ by 48¾ inches. The Huntington Gallery, San Marino, CA.

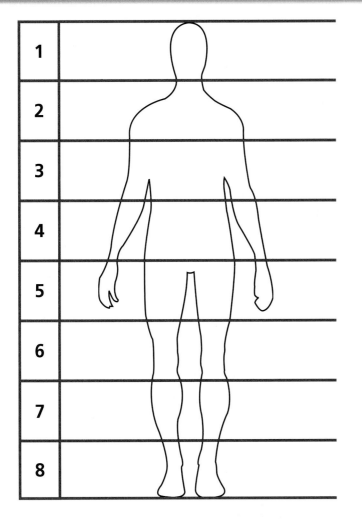

1	
2	
3	
4	
5	
6	
7	
8	

This proportion grid shows adult proportions.

Just as artists look at proportions when drawing faces, they also pay attention to proportions when drawing an entire figure. A grid for an adult figure shows that the body is approximately eight "heads" tall. A grid for a child's figure should show only about six head lengths.

Art Fact

The ancient Roman architect Vitruvius created a model of the human body with what he thought were ideal proportions. Leonardo da Vinci used those measurements too.

Show Proportion

Draw a portrait of a classmate. Measure how many head lengths you will need for the height.

1 Draw the form of your model's body. Use a grid to show realistic proportions.

2 Paint the figure in your drawing.

Technique Tip

Look at the illustration on page 177. Then use the size of your subject's head to figure out proportions of other body parts.

3 Add details to show the clothing, face, and hair.

4 Add a familiar indoor or outdoor setting around the figure.

Think Like an Artist

Does your portrait capture the posture and proportions of your model? What would you do differently in your next portrait painting?

Stage Designs

José González says it takes a team to put on a play. He is a stage designer, or a person who plans a play's set—the painted backgrounds, the furniture, and other scenery.

González starts planning a stage design by reading the playscript. He meets with the director and the lighting and costume designers. They share ideas and agree on a general "look" for the play. Then González makes sketches of his stage design ideas.

González often builds three-dimensional models of his designs. He starts with a simple white model. Later he adds details and color so everyone can see how the set will look during the play. González believes that a successful stage design helps move along the action of the play.

González had to learn many skills to get his job. He had no experience designing stages when he first worked on a stage set years ago. He apprenticed, or learned on the job, for weeks without pay. Now, González is Executive Director of a theater group in Oregon. What he likes best about his job is seeing an idea come to life.

José González designs sets for the Miracle Theatre Group in Portland, Oregon.

González used the model shown above to plan this stage design.

Design a Cartoon Car

Combine your new skills as a cartoonist and industrial designer. Design a car for your favorite cartoon character.

1

Design a car for a cartoon character.

2

Add details to your car.

3

Draw your favorite cartoon character in or near the car.

4

Complete your car by gluing on pipe cleaners, nuts, bolts, and other mechanical parts.

Paige, Age 9. *Rabbit Mobile.*
Markers, pipe cleaners, bottlecaps,
and mechanical parts on paper.

How are these students' car
designs attractive and useful?

Sophie, Age 9. *Star Car.* Markers,
pipe cleaners, bottlecaps, and
mechanical parts on paper.

Share Your Art

1. Would you describe your car as modern or old-
   fashioned? Explain.

2. What makes the car design well-suited to your
   cartoon character?

Think About Art

Read the art words. Then explain how one of the pictures relates to that term.

tradition   cartoon   weft

proportion   industrial design   portrait

Write About Art

What can artists today learn from the past? Write your ideas.

Talk About Art

- Choose an artwork from your portfolio that shows a contrast with traditional art forms.
- Tell why you think the artwork is successful.
- Explain what you tried to show in this artwork. Use words you learned in this unit.

Red Grooms. *Dali Salad,* 1980–1981. Color lithograph and silkscreen, cut out, glued, and mounted on rag paper (edition of 55), 26½ by 27½ by 12 inches. Courtesy Brooke Alexander Gallery, Inc., New York. Photograph © D. James Dee, New York. © 1998 Red Grooms/Artists Rights Society (ARS), New York.

Put It All Together

1. Describe the subject of the artwork.

2. What makes this three-dimensional portrait unusual?

3. Do you think this artwork is serious or humorous? Explain.

4. Would you like to own this artwork? Explain.

Carmen Lomas Garza. *Haciendo Papel Picado/Making Paper Cutouts,* 1998. Black paper cutout, 22 by 30 inches. Collection of Carmen Lomas Garza, San Francisco, CA. © 1998 Carmen Lomas Garza.

An Assortment of Art

You have read about various art forms and media, both old and new. In this unit, you will see a few more interesting art styles and materials.

Some artworks express the artist's cultural background. This artwork shows people making **cut-paper art,** a traditional Mexican art form called *papel picado.*

Meet the Artist

Much of the work of artist Carmen Lomas Garza shows special and everyday events in the lives of some Mexican Americans. Garza's artworks also appear as illustrations in books she has written. These children's books are based mostly on Garza's childhood in Texas. Find more *papel picado* by Garza later in this unit.

Mixed-Media Artworks

Sometimes artists use **mixed media** to express themselves. In mixed-media artworks, artists create with more than one medium. These artists may use their cultural heritage as the **theme,** or main message, of their artwork.

Faith Ringgold. *Harlem Renaissance Party: Bitter Nest, Part II,* 1988. Acrylic on canvas, printed, tie-dyed, and pieced fabric, 94 by 82 inches. © 1988 Faith Ringgold, Inc.

Miriam Schapiro. *Mechano/Flower Fan,* 1979. Acrylic and fabric collage on paper, 30 by 44 inches. The National Museum of Women in the Arts, Washington, D.C. Gift of Mary Ross Taylor, in honor of her mother, W. B. Abbott.

Faith Ringgold's **story quilt** combines fabric and paint to tell a story. It shows famous people who created a community of artists during a time known as the Harlem Renaissance. The words along the border tell their story.

Miriam Schapiro describes her art as **femmage,** a collage of fabrics traditionally made by women. What would you use in a collage to call attention to your interests? Why?

Sketchbook Journal

Think about a story you want to tell in a mixed-media artwork. Make a list of materials you could use, and illustrate your list. Draw a sketch of your theme.

Studio 1

Design a Story Quilt

What story could you use as the subject of a story quilt? Think about design elements to include.

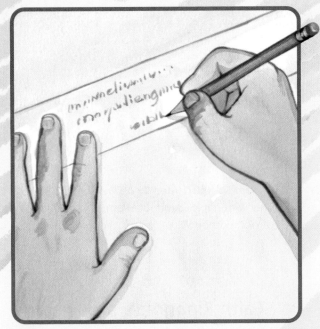

1 Choose a story that would make a good subject for a story quilt.

 2 Begin writing a story along the borders of a sheet of paper.

Technique Tip

Cover the border with paper as you illustrate the center to avoid smearing your writing.

 3 Decorate the border with colorful details as you write.

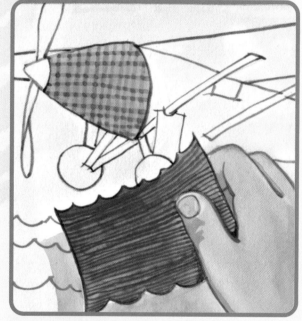

4 Choose a new medium to illustrate the story in the center of the quilt.

Think Like an Artist

Describe how the illustrations in the center complement the words around the border.

Relief Sculpture

Relief sculpture is a form of art that is thousands of years old. Parts of a relief sculpture are raised to make them stand out from a flat background. The relief in this sculpture was created by carving away the background areas.

Artist unknown. *The Goddess Hathor and King Sethi,* ca. 1294–1279 B.C. Painted limestone relief. Musée du Louvre, Paris.

The ancient Egyptian artwork shown here is a relief sculpture.

Artist unknown. *Harpist,* ca. 1800 B.C. Terra-cotta plaque, 3 by 4⅗ inches. Musée du Louvre, Paris.

Notice how the head in the Egyptian relief sculpture is shown in **profile,** or from a side view. However, the body faces forward. This style was used in Egyptian art for thousands of years.

Compare the terra-cotta relief sculpture above with the Egyptian sculpture. Talk about similarities and differences in how the figures are portrayed.

Sketchbook Journal

How would an Egyptian artist have portrayed you? Draw a picture of yourself as a figure in an Egyptian relief sculpture. Describe and explain the point of view.

Make a Relief Sculpture

Follow these steps to turn a three-dimensional collage of a historical person into a relief sculpture.

1 Make a sketch of a person from history. Draw from memory or imagination.

2 Glue cut cardboard and found objects to create a relief sculpture.

Technique Tip

Build the relief material up to one inch deep. Press the foil gently with a pencil eraser to form the relief.

3 After the portrait dries, brush thinned white glue over the entire surface.

4 Starting from the center, gently press a sheet of foil over the entire portrait.

Think Like an Artist

Explain how successful you were in creating the flat and raised forms that you planned. Does your relief sculpture have light and dark areas?

Many Kinds of Folk Art

Do you know someone who whittles wooden toys, makes decorative quilts, or carves birds? If so, you probably know a **folk artist,** a self-taught artist. Folk artists create artworks, called **folk art,** that often reflect the artists' cultural symbols and beliefs.

David Moctezuma. *Alebreje,* 2003. Papier-mâché, 6 by 10 inches. Milagros Mexican Folk Art, Seattle, WA.

Clark Coe. *Killingworth Image, Man on a Hog,* ca. 1890. Carved, assembled, and painted wood, tinned iron, and textile remnants, 37 by 38 by 21⅜ inches. Smithsonian American Art Museum, Washington, D.C.

This mixed-media sculpture is another example of folk art.

The Linares family of Mexico is known for its folk art **papier-mâché** sculptures. Paper strips are dipped in a watery paste and added in layers to an **armature,** or frame. It provides strength and shape. The grandfather, Pedro Linares, first made the sculptures. Now other family members, such as David Moctezuma, create these imaginative works as well.

Sketchbook Journal

Draw a picture of an unusually colorful fish or animal from memory, observation, or your imagination. Write a plan to create the sculpture based on your drawing.

Studio 3

Create Papier-Mâché

Design your own papier-mâché sculpture of an animal, a person, a plant, or an imaginary figure.

1 Form an armature using wire, an inflated balloon, or wadded-up newspaper.

2 Dip newspaper strips into paste and remove excess. Lay strips on armature.

Technique Tip

Use wide newspaper strips to cover wide forms. Thin strips will lie flat on small areas. Let each layer dry before you add another.

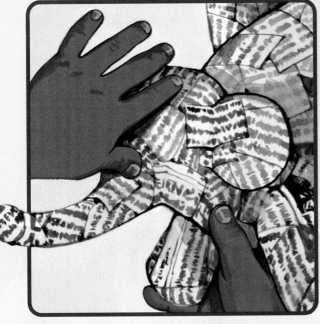

3 Continue adding strips until the main form is finished. Shape details.

4 After the paper dries, paint the sculpture. Add found objects for decoration.

Think Like an Artist

Would you describe your papier-mâché sculpture as folk art? Explain.

Cultural Scenes

Grandma Moses created scenes of New England traditions long before Carmen Lomas Garza began to paint scenes of her own Mexican American culture. Unlike Garza, however, Grandma Moses did not begin to paint until she was in her seventies.

Carmen Lomas Garza. *Barbacoa para Cumpleaños (Birthday Barbecue),* 1993. Alkyds on canvas, 36 by 48 inches. Collection of Federal Reserve Bank of Dallas, Dallas, TX. © 1993 Carmen Lomas Garza (reg. 1994).

Grandma Moses. *Joy Ride,* 1953. Oil on pressed wood, 18 by 24 inches. © 1992, Grandma Moses Properties Co., New York.

Compare the subjects, styles, and cultures shown in these two paintings. Point out how each artist showed pattern and rhythm. What part of each painting does your eye go to first?

Which painting shows warm weather? Which one shows cold weather? How can you tell?

Research

Find a picture of either *Children's Games* or *Winter Scene* by Pieter Brueghel. Compare the Brueghel painting with either *Birthday Barbecue* or *Joy Ride.*

Fiber Art

Many artists create useful objects, such as blankets, rugs, or baskets, by hand. They make **fiber art,** art created with thread or thread-like materials.

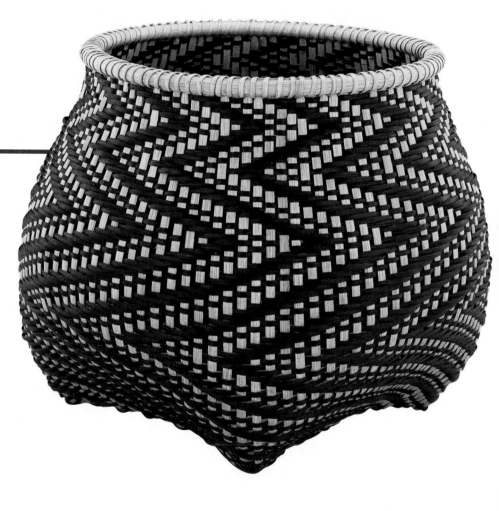

Billie Ruth Sudduth. *Fibonacci 5*, 1996. Hand-shaped and hand-dyed reed splints, with twill weave construction, 13 by 16½ inches. Smithsonian American Art Museum, Washington, D.C.

Artist unknown, African. *Raffia Cloth*, ca. 1935. Embroidered cut pile. Gerard Foundation Collection, Museum of International Folk Art, Santa Fe, NM. Photo by Michel Monteaux.

The basket artist used natural fibers to weave an object that is both beautiful and useful. Sometimes baskets are woven so tightly that they can hold water.

The cloth weaving above is a **raffia cloth.** It is woven from raffia, a fiber that is also used to make baskets.

How are the texture and designs on these two objects similar?

Art in My World

Look around your home, classroom, or community. See how many ways people use baskets, a traditional fiber craft object seen in many parts of the world. Describe the design of a basket.

Weave Natural Objects

Weavers use looms of many shapes and sizes. Try this fiber art project using a branch for a loom.

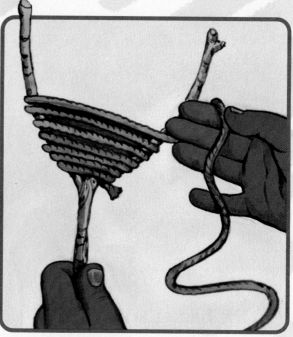

1 Find a small tree branch that is shaped like the letter *Y*.

2 Wrap yarn around the outer parts of the *Y* for the warp.

Technique Tip

Wrap the warp tightly around each side of the *Y* so it will not slip. Knot the beginning and end of the warp.

3 Next, weave in various fibers to make the weft. Do not pull the weft too tight.

4 Use your fingertips to adjust the spacing of the warp and weft.

Think Like an Artist

Explain why an artist might make a weaving like yours instead of one on a traditional loom. How did you consider unity and color in your weaving?

Murals

You might see a **mural** in almost any big city in the United States. These large artworks are usually painted directly on a ceiling or a wall in a public place. Some murals are indoors. Others decorate outdoor spaces.

Yreina D. Cervantez. *La Ofrenda (The Offering),* 1990. Mural. Los Angeles, CA. Commissioned by SPARC, through its Great Walls Unlimited: Neighborhood Pride Program. Photo courtesy of SPARC (www.sparcmurals.org).

Describe some details you see in this mural. What elements of art did the artist use to create unity and variety?

John Steuart Curry. (Detail) *Kansas Pastoral.* Mural at the Kansas State House, Topeka, KS.

What can you learn about Kansas from Curry's mural? What values do you think Curry wanted to reflect?

Muralists often use their artwork to tell a story about something important to them. What story do you think these **muralists** wanted to show?

Sometimes murals are painted by one person. At other times a group of muralists works together to design and create a mural. The mural above was designed by one artist. How does the credit line reflect this information?

Sketchbook Journal

Draw a place in your community where you think a mural would look just right. What story would the mural tell? Write a list of words for your story.

Studio 5
Make a Mural

Take your place in history. Help create a mural for a wall in your school.

1 Work with your group to brainstorm and draw ideas for a mural.

2 Combine the sketches and make a grid of one-inch squares over the sketch.

Technique Tip

Fill in one square at a time when transferring the sketch. Match each square on the mural with the same square in the original sketch.

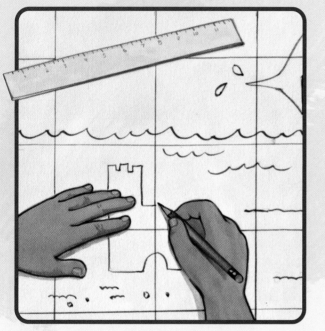

3 Draw a grid of six-inch squares on craft paper. Transfer the original sketch.

4 Choose jobs. Who will prepare, paint, and clean up?

Think Like an Artist

How did you create unity among the different parts of your mural?

Mosaics

Artists have made **mosaics** for thousands of years. A mosaic is like a puzzle. It is made of small bits of material, usually tile, glass, or stone, called **tesserae.** The artist creates a design by arranging and gluing the tesserae.

Artist unknown.
Byzantine Emperor.
Mosaic.

Antonio Gaudí. *Güell Park,* Barcelona, Spain.

Gaudí spent fourteen years constructing Güell Park in Barcelona, Spain.

In ancient Rome, mosaics, such as the one shown on page 210, decorated a wall or floor. Notice how the artist used heavy dark lines to emphasize facial features.

Gaudí used mosaics to cover sculptures, benches, and other three-dimensional structures in this park. Why do you think the mosaics glitter in the light?

Art Fact

Many mosaics were found in good shape when ash from a volcanic eruption was cleared away from the ancient city of Pompeii in Italy. The volcano erupted in A.D. 79.

Make a Paper Mosaic

Try this version of the ancient art of mosaic.

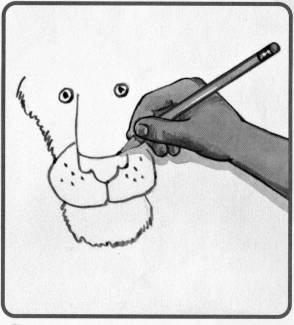

1 Sort your paper bits, or tesserae, by color, size, and shape.

2 Draw the outline of a design that you like.

Technique Tip

Glue tesserae from the center of the design outward. Leave a little space between the tesserae.

3 Put glue on the paper and place the tesserae one at a time.

4 Continue gluing down the tesserae until your design is complete.

Think Like an Artist

How could you add more relief to the surface of your mosaic? Name some objects you could use in place of a few tesserae.

Comic Illustrations

How do artists make comic books? Illustrator Stan Webb follows many steps. First, he conducts research. Webb works with a writer to study the subject. Then, he and the writer do much thinking and planning to develop the characters.

Finally, the writer writes the story. Webb draws the illustrations, then scans them into a computer and adds color. It takes about thirty days for Webb to illustrate one comic book.

Webb's favorite part of the process is drawing the characters. He enjoys making them seem like real people. According to Webb, the best comic books combine two traits. He values great story-telling and great illustrations with a lot of action and details. What characteristics do *you* value in a comic book?

Stan Webb, comic book illustrator

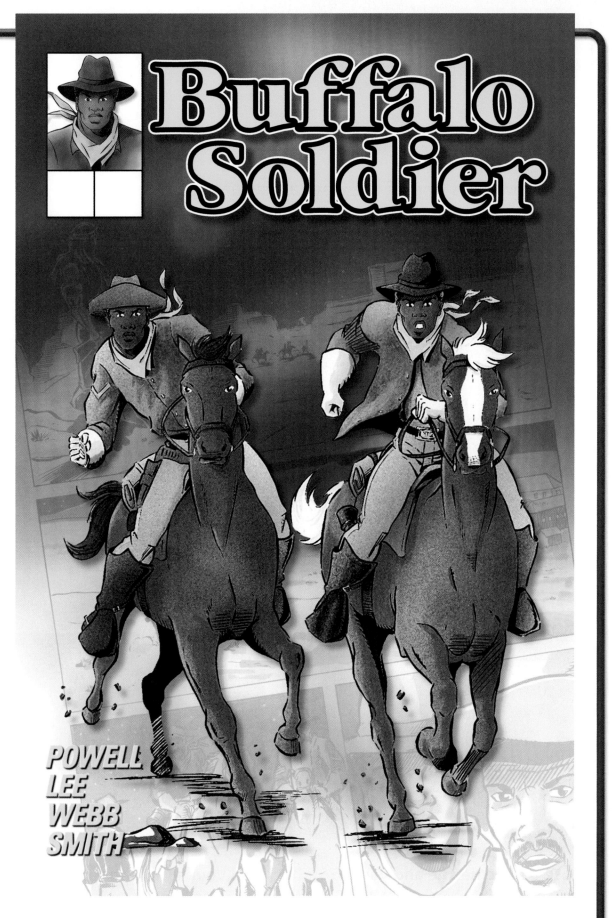

What do you think this comic book's story is about?

Stitch Your Own Design

Needlework is one of the ways artists around the world express their creativity. Add your creative square to a class quilt.

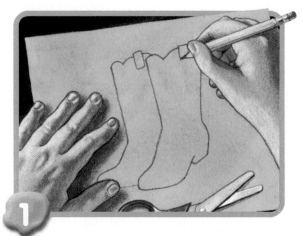

1 Draw a design that has your initials and a symbol of a way you express yourself.

2 Cut out your design and transfer it onto a square of burlap.

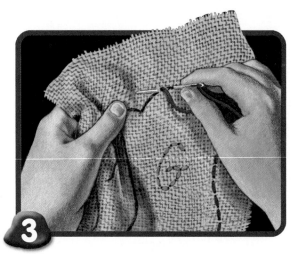

3 Use a large needle and yarn to stitch over the initials and symbol you drew.

4 Add your square to those of your classmates to form a quilt.

Timothy, Age 10, and Joseph, Age 9. *Baseball Is the Best!* and *Reading is Fun.* Burlap and yarn.

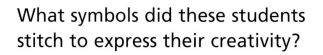

Henry, Age 9, and Jennifer, Age 10. *Drums* and *Plants.* Burlap and yarn.

What symbols did these students stitch to express their creativity?

Share Your Art

1. What is the theme of your stitchery?

2. Could your class quilt be described as both a story quilt and a work of fiber art? Explain.

Think About Art

Point to a picture that matches each word. Explain how the picture illustrates what the word means.

fiber art	theme	folk art
mosaic	relief sculpture	mural

Comic Mosaic Mask,
A.D. 1st century.

Tomb Guardian,
A.D. 1000–1470.

Write About Art

Which of the new art forms that you explored in this unit was the most interesting and unusual? Describe it, and explain your choice.

Talk About Art

- Look through your portfolio.
- Choose an artwork that surprised you in some way.
- Tell a friend what you discovered by making it.
- Explain what you learned in this unit that you tried to show in this artwork.

Artist unknown, Navajo culture, Arizona. *Blanket: Map of the Four Corners Area,* ca. 1960. Tapestry-woven wool, 38 by 29¼ inches. From the Girard Foundation Collection, in the Museum of International Folk Art, a unit of the Museum of New Mexico, Santa Fe, NM.

Put It All Together

1. What is this weaving about?

2. How did the artist show both unity and variety?

3. What theme do you think the weaver had in mind?

4. Do you think this weaving should be considered folk art? Explain.

Line

straight

curved

zigzag

thin

thick

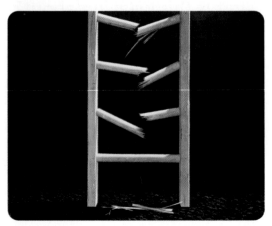

broken

Color

cool

warm

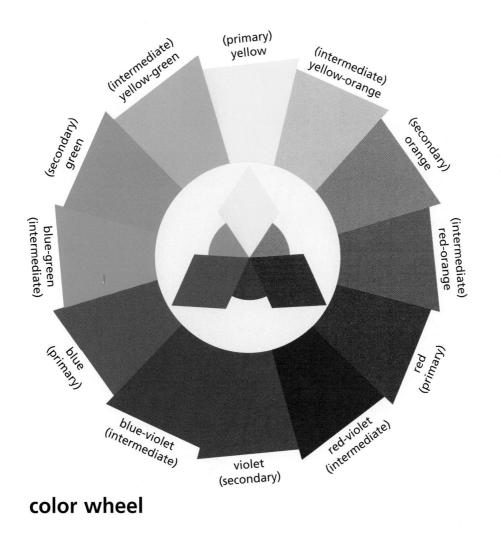

color wheel

Value

Shape

geometric shapes | organic shapes

Texture

bumpy

soft

shiny

prickly

sticky

fluffy

224

Form

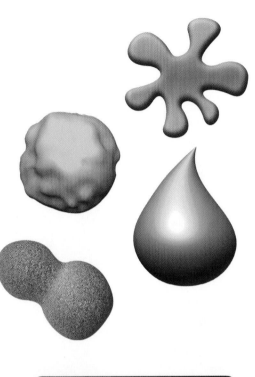

geometric forms

organic forms

Space

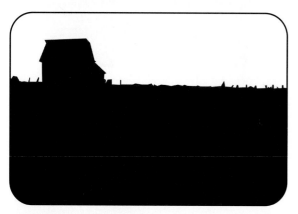

positive space

negative space

Unity

Principles of Design

Variety

Emphasis

Principles of Design

Balance

Proportion

Pattern

Rhythm

Think Safety

Read these safety rules. Be sure to follow these rules when you create artworks.

1. Keep art materials away from your face, especially your mouth and eyes.

2. Be careful when you work with scissors. If you use a sharp object, point it away from your body.

3. Read the labels on art materials. Look for the word *nontoxic*. This label tells you the materials are safe to use.

4. Do not breathe chalk dust or art sprays.

5. If you have a problem with any art materials, ask your teacher for help.

6. If an art material makes you feel sick, tell your teacher right away.

7. If you spill water or paint on the floor, be sure to clean it up quickly. A wet floor is unsafe to walk on.

8. Clean up after you finish an artwork. First, wash your hands with soap and water. Then, wash the tools you want to save, such as paintbrushes. Return art materials to their proper places.

Can you think of more ways to be safe?

List of Artists

List of Artists

Glossary

A

abstract [ab strakt´] A style of art in which the subject of an artwork has been simplified or rearranged. Abstract art emphasizes moods and impressions and is characterized by the use of bold colors, lines, and flat shapes.

actual line A line that is real. It is a line you can actually see.

analogous [ə na´ lə gəs] The name given to colors that are next to each other on the color wheel (for example, yellow, yellow-orange, and orange). They are also called *related colors*.

animation The process of showing in rapid succession a series of drawings or photographs, each image having a small change in the position of the subject(s). This process creates the illusion of motion.

architect [är´ ka tekt] A professional who designs buildings.

architecture [är´ kə tek chər] The art and science of designing buildings and other large-scale, functional structures.

armature [är´ mə chùr] In sculpture, a framework used to support material, such as clay or papier-mâché, that is being formed.

assemblage [ə sem´ blij] A type of three-dimensional art created by combining and connecting a variety of objects to create a pleasing whole.

asymmetrical [ā sə me´ tri kəl] **balance** A type of balance in which two sides of an artwork are not alike but carry equal or nearly equal visual weight. It is also known as *informal balance*.

asymmetry [ā si´ mə trē] A type of balance that lacks symmetry.

B

background The part of an artwork that appears to be farthest from the viewer, often in the distance of a scene.

balance The arrangement of the parts of an artwork to give an overall sense of equality in visual weight. Balance can be symmetrical, asymmetrical, or radial. Balance is a principle of design.

basket A hollow vessel created by weaving together stiff fibers such as twigs or reeds.

blueprint A large print of an architectural plan shown with white lines on a blue background.

brayer [brā´ ər] In printing, a rubber roller used to spread ink over a surface.

cartoon A drawing, as in a newspaper or magazine, intended to amuse the reader. A cartoon often has a caption.

cartoon character A person, animal, or thing shown in an artwork that is humorous. Words often go with the drawings.

cartoon strip A series of cartoon drawings that tell a story.

center of interest The part of an artwork the viewer notices first. It is the most important part of an artwork.

ceramic [sə ra´ mik] A hard material made by baking, or firing, clay. It is also the artwork made of the ceramic.

clay A powdery substance found in the earth that becomes pliable, or flexible, when moistened and hardens when baked. Clay is used to create artworks such as sculpture and pottery.

collage [kə läzh´] An artwork created by arranging and gluing small pictures or photographs, pieces of paper, fabric, or other materials, onto a larger, flat surface.

Jane Sterrett. *Diversity Collage.*

color The visual quality of objects, as they reflect hues on the color wheel, caused by the amount of light reflected by them. Color is an element of art.

color scheme A plan for combining color in an artwork.

complementary colors Colors that contrast strongly with one another and are directly across from one another on the color wheel.

composition [käm pə zi´ shən] The arrangement of the various parts of an artwork into a pleasing whole. Composition also refers to a work of art.

contrast To show a large difference between two elements of art.

cool colors Related colors that range from green through blue and violet. Cool colors often bring to mind cool objects, places, and feelings.

cut-paper art (papel picado) Traditional Mexican art of cutting decorative and patterned designs into sheets of tissue paper.

D

decorative art A handicraft that results in beautiful, useful objects. Rug and fabric design, furniture-making, and glassblowing are all decorative arts.

detail A small part of an artwork that has been pulled out and usually enlarged for close inspection. A detail is also a tiny or particularly interesting part of an artwork.

diagonal line A line that slants in one direction. A diagonal line is neither vertical nor horizontal.

E

elements of art The basic parts of an artwork, including line, color, value, shape, texture, form, and space.

emphasis [em´ fə səs] The visual accent, stress, or sense of importance created in an artwork by the color, size, shape, or placement of an object or area. Emphasis is a principle of design.

Expressionistic [ik spre shə nis´ tik] A style of art in which the artist boldly expresses personal experiences and emotions about a subject using simple designs and brillant colors. Expressionism began in Germany during the early 1900s. It became popular in the United States during the 1940s and 1950s.

Eye-Dazzler Blanket A blanket woven in a specific and traditional Navajo style, with intricate patterns of bright colors.

F

fantasy Refers to art made from the creative imagination.

femmage [fem´ äzh] A type of collage made by women that usually includes vintage fabric items sewn and used by women.

fiber art Artwork created from yarn, thread, or cloth. Stitchery and weaving are examples of fiber art.

Artist unknown. *Otal avo Indian Weaving* (Detail).

firing Baking clay in a kiln. Firing causes the clay to retain its hardness.

floor plan A drawing that shows the arrangement of rooms in a building, as seen from a bird's-eye view.

folk art Artwork that often reflects traditions of a particular culture, especially images made by artists who do not have formal training. Instead, they are usually self-taught or learn from their friends and relatives.

foreground The part of an artwork that appears to be nearest the viewer.

form A three-dimensional object, such as a cube or a sphere, that is shown in three-dimensional artworks. Form is defined by height, depth, and width and is an element of art.

functional art Art created and used for a specific purpose.

G

geometric shape A shape that is mathematically defined or regular in appearance, such as a triangle, circle, square, or rectangle.

glaze A glassy substance that is applied to clay before firing in a kiln. It forms a hard surface that can protect the clay and serve as decoration.

Artist unknown. *Horse*, 8th Century.

H

horizontal line A line that is straight and flat, parallel to the horizon.

hue [hyü´] Another word for color.

I

implied line A line that is not shown but is implied, or suggested, by the placement of other lines, shapes, and colors.

industrial design The design of objects, such as automobiles, appliances, and telephones, manufactured and sold by industry.

installation An artwork asembled for an exhibition and dissambled when the exhibition is over.

intermediate color A color created when a primary color (yellow, red, or blue) is mixed with a secondary color (orange, violet, or green). Some examples are red-violet and blue-green.

J

jewelry [jü′ əl rē] Ornaments or decorative objects that people wear, such as rings, bracelets, and necklaces. Artists design and make jewelry.

K

kiln A hot oven used to bake and harden artworks made of clay, such as pottery or ceramics.

L

landscape An artwork showing an outdoor scene or scenery.

line The thin path of a point, usually created by a pen, pencil, or paintbrush. Lines can be actual or implied. A line can be thick or thin and can be curved, straight, zigzag, wavy, spiral, or broken. Line is an element of art.

loom [lüm′] A frame-like tool used to hold fibers for weaving fabric.

M

mask An artwork made to be placed over a person's face for disguise and decoration.

media [mē′ dē ə] The materials used to create artworks, such as charcoal, pastels, oil paints, or clay. Media also refers to the techniques used to make an artwork, such as painting, sculpting, or drawing. The singular of *media* is *medium*.

middle ground The part of an artwork that appears to lie between the foreground and the background.

mixed media Artworks created by using more than one medium. For example, collage can be a mixed-media artwork in which drawing, painting, and photography are combined.

model Someone or something the artist uses as an example when creating an artwork. Also, in architecture, a model is a small version that represents a larger building or structure.

monument A three-dimensional artwork created to honor a person or an event.

mosaic [mō zā′ ik] An artwork created by setting tesserae into mortar or onto another adhesive background to create a unified pattern or image. See *tesserae*.

motion picture A series of slightly changing images recorded on a filmstrip. When viewed in rapid succession, the rapidly changing images create the illusion of continuous motion.

movement In an artwork, a quality that evokes a sense of action, often created using lines or patterns.

mural [myùr′ əl] A large artwork, usually a painting, applied to a wall or ceiling. Murals often appear on or in public buildings.

N

negative space The empty space that surrounds a form or shape in an artwork.

neutrals [nü′ trəls] A term used for black, white, and tints and shades of gray. Some artists also consider browns to be neutral.

nonobjective [nän əb jek′ tiv] **style** A term used to describe artworks that have no recognizable subject matter. This style does not represent real objects.

object Something in an artwork that usually can be named by the viewer.

organic shape Shapes and forms that are irregular, particularly those resembling objects in nature, such as the shape of a leaf or the form of an animal.

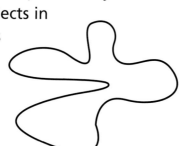

overlap To partly or completely cover one shape or form with another.

P

papier-mâché [pā pər mə shā'] A material made from paper pulp that can be molded when wet and painted when dry. It is also the technique for making sculptures from this material.

pattern Repetition of color, line, shape, or form in an artwork. Pattern is a principle of design. Also, a pattern is a plan or model to be followed when making something.

photography The art of creating photographs.

plate See *printing block*.

Pop Art A style of art developed during the 1950s. Pop Artists show people, objects, or scenes from popular culture and use graphics similar to those found in advertisements or comic strips.

portrait [pōr' trət] An artwork that features a person, an animal, or a group of people, often placing emphasis on the face.

Christian Pierre. *Troy*, 1962.

pose The way people or animals sit or stand while an artist creates a portrait of them.

positive space Shapes, forms, or lines that stand out from the background or negative space in an artwork.

primary color One of the three colors (yellow, red, and blue) from which other colors are made

principles of design Guidelines artists use to arrange elements of art. The principles of design are unity, variety, emphasis, balance, proportion, pattern, and rhythm.

print An artwork created by coating a surface, such as a carved wood block, with wet color and then pressing paper onto it. The paper is "pulled" as a print.

244

printing block A surface, such as wood or linoleum, into which an artist carves a design. Ink or paint is spread across the surface and paper is pressed onto it to make a print, an impression of the design.

printmaker A person who creates prints, or multiple images, by using the same printing block.

profile Something that is seen or shown from the side, such as a side view of a face.

proportion [prə pōr´ shən] The size relationship of one part of an artwork to another part or to the whole. For example, the size relationship of the nose to the face shows proportion. Proportion is a principle of design.

quilt A padded bedcover made from two layers of cloth that are sewn together. Usually, one layer is made from

scraps of fabric that have been arranged and stitched together in a colorful design. Also, the term is used to mean creating a quilt.

quilt block A section of a quilt top, usually square or rectangular.

R

radial [rā´ dē əl] **balance** A type of balance in which lines or shapes spread out from a center point.

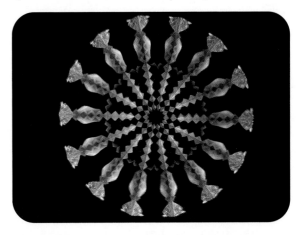

raffia [ra´ fē ə] **cloth** Cloth woven from the leaf fibers of the raffia, an African palm tree.

realistic A style of art that describes artworks showing objects and scenes as they actually look to most viewers.

relief [ri lēf´] **print** An artwork made by rolling ink onto a carved surface showing a raised design and then pressing paper onto it.

relief sculpture [ri lēf´ skəlp´ chər] A kind of sculpture that stands out from a flat background.

rhythm [ri´ thəm] A sense of visual movement or motion caused by the repetition of one or more elements of art, such as color, line, shape, or form, in an artwork. Rhythm is a principle of design.

S

sculpture [skəlp´ chər] An artwork made by modeling, carving, or joining materials into a three-dimensional whole. Clay, wood, stone, and metal are some common materials used for sculpture. Sculpture is also the process of making such an artwork.

secondary color A color created by mixing two primary colors. The secondary colors are orange (made from yellow and red), violet (made from red and blue), and green (made from blue and yellow).

self-portrait [self´ pōr´ trət] An artwork showing a likeness of the artist who created it.

shade A darker value created by adding black to a color or by adding black to white.

shading A way of showing gradual changes of darker values in an artwork. Shading helps make a flat artwork appear three-dimensional.

shape A two-dimensional flat area made by lines that enclose it. A shape can be geometric, such as a circle or square, or organic, having an irregular outline. Shape is an element of art.

space The open or empty area around, above, between, within, or below objects. Shapes and forms are defined by the empty space surrounding them (negative space) and by the space they occupy (positive space). Space is an element of art.

still life An artwork showing an arrangement of objects that do not move on their own.

still photograph A photograph that does not move, as compared to a motion picture.

story quilt A quilt showing pictures and words that tell a story.

style An artist's own special way of creating art through the use of specific media, methods, materials, or subjects. Artistic style can also represent certain techniques of a group of artists in a specific culture or time.

subject What an artwork is about. It can be a person, object, or scene. A subject is the recognizable topic of an artwork.

symbol [sim´bəl] A letter, color, sign, or picture used to represent a word, message, or idea.

symmetrical [sə me´tri kəl] **balance** A type of balance in which both sides of a center line are the same or about the same. A cat's face, for example, is symmetrically balanced along a vertical line through the middle of the nose. Symmetrical balance is also known as *formal balance*.

symmetry [si´mə trē] Balance created by making both sides of an artwork the same or about the same.

tactile texture [tak´təl teks´chər] Texture that can be understood by the sense of touch. It is also called *actual texture*. Tactile textures, which artists show in their compositions, include rough, smooth, silky, pebbly, soft, hard, bumpy, and scratchy. See *texture*.

technology The way human beings use machines and other tools to make or do something. Technology in art helps artists solve problems in making and doing art.

tesserae [te´sə rə] In a mosaic, the small pieces of glass, tile, stones, paper, or similar material set into mortar or onto another adhesive surface to create a unified pattern. See *mosaic*.

Artist unknown. Roman. Mosaic-Two Roman Figures.

texture [teks´chər] The way a surface feels (actual or tactile texture) or looks (visual texture). Words such as shiny, dull, rough, and smooth are used to describe texture. Texture is an element of art.

theme The artist's particular interpretation of a broad or abstract topic, such as nature, love, or beauty.

three-dimensional Having height, width, and depth or thickness. Something that is three-dimensional is not a flat shape. It is a form.

tint A light value of a color created by mixing the color with white.

traditional style A style that conforms to knowledge, beliefs, and customs passed down from one generation to the next. See *style*.

two-dimensional Having height and width but not depth. Something that is two-dimensional is flat.

unity [yü′ nə tē] A quality that occurs when all parts of an artwork combine to create a sense of wholeness and completion. Unity is a principle of design.

value [val′ yü] The lightness or darkness of a color. Tints have a light value. Shades have a dark value. For example, pink is a light value of red, while navy is a dark value of blue. Value is an element of art.

variety [və rī′ ə tē] The combination of elements of art, such as line, shape, or color, that adds interest to an artwork. Variety is a principle of design.

vertical line A line that goes straight up and down.

visual texture
[vi′ zhə wəl teks′ chər] The way a surface appears through the sense of vision. For example, the surface of a sculpture may be shiny or dull. See *texture*.

warm colors The family of related colors that range from yellow through orange and red. Warm colors usually remind people of warm objects, places, and feelings.

warp [wȯrp′] In weaving, fibers stretched vertically, top to bottom, on a loom and through which the weft is woven.

weave [wēv′] To make cloth-like artworks by interlacing, or weaving, warp and weft threads, or other fiber, often on a loom.

weft In weaving, fibers woven over and under, from side to side, through the warp on a loom.

Index

Index

Acknowledgments

ILLUSTRATIONS

20, 21, 24, 25, 28, 29, 34, 35, 38, 39, 42, 43, 54, 55, 58, 59, 62, 63, 68, 69, 72, 73, 76, 77, 88. 89, 92, 93, 96, 97, 102, 103, 105, 106, 107, 110, 111, 122, 123, 126, 127, 130, 131, 136, 137, 140, 141, 144, 145, 156, 157, 160, 161, 164, 165, 170, 171, 174, 175, 178, 179, 182, 190, 191, 194, 195, 198, 199, 204, 205, 208, 209, 212, 213, 216 Carol Newsom

46, 80, 114, 148 Connie McLennan

PHOTOGRAPHS

Every effort has been made to secure permission and provide appropriate credit for photographic material. The publisher deeply regrets any omission and pledges to correct errors called to its attention in subsequent editions.

Unless otherwise acknowledged, all photographs are the property of Scott Foresman, a division of Pearson Education.

Photo locators denoted as follows: Top (t), Center (c), Bottom (b), Left (l), Right (r), Background (Bkgd)

Front Matter

Page 7, © SuperStock; 7, Sisse Brimberg, © National Geographic; 10, © Smithsonian American Art Museum, Washington, D.C./Art Resource, NY; 14, © Erich Lessing/Art Resource, NY. © 2004 Estate of Pablo Picasso/Artists Rights Society (ARS), New York.

Units 1–6

Page 16, © Réunion des Musées Nationaux/Art Resource, NY; 17, Claude Monet. *Self-Portrait,* 1917. Oil on canvas, 27 1/3 by 21 1/2 inches. Musée d'Orsay, Paris, France. © Erich Lessing/Art Resource, NY; 30, © Francis G. Mayer/Corbis; 32, Photo by Doug Parker Studios, courtesy of Frank Romero; 37, © Corbis; 40, Fine Arts Museums of San Francisco, Achenbach Foundation for Graphic Arts, Gift of Mr. and Mrs. Robert Marcus,1990.1.116; 44 (tr), © Toba Garrett; 44 (bc), 45, Photography by Steven Mark Needham, cake photo courtesy of The Well Decorated Cake, © 2003/Courtesy of Sterling Publishing; 48, © Getty Images, 48, © Frans Lemmens/Getty Images; 48, © Corbis; 49, © 2004 Artists Rights Society (ARS), New York/VG Bild Kunst, Bonn.; 50, © 2004 Jacob Lawrence Foundation/Artists Rights Society (ARS), New York; 51, Collection of the National Academy of Design, New York, NY. © 2004 Jacob Lawrence Foundation/Artists Rights Society (ARS), New York; 56, © Fiduciario en el Fideicomiso relativo a los Museos Diego Rivera y Frida Kahlo. Reproduction authorized by the Bank of Mexico, Mexico City; 60, The Baltimore Museum of Art, The Cone Collection, formed by Dr. Claribel Cone and Miss Etta Cone of Baltimore, Maryland BMA 1950.196; 61(tr), © Corbis; 64, © Smithsonian American Art Museum, Washington, D.C./Art Resource, NY. © 2004 Jacob Lawrence Foundation/Artists Rights Society (ARS), New York; 65, Toledo Museum of Art, purchased with funds from the Libbey Endowment, gift of Edward Drummond Libbey, 1976.34. © Richard Estes/Toledo Museum of Art; 67, © Adam Woolfitt/Corbis; 67, © Bob London/Corbis; 70, Collection of the American Folk Art Museum, New York; 71, © Peter Harholdt/SuperStock; 78, 79, © Annamaree Rea; 82, © Peter Harholdt/SuperStock; 82, © Burstein Collection/Corbis; 83, © SuperStock; 84, © 2004 Estate of Louise Nevelson/Artists Rights Society (ARS), New York; 85, Hans Namuth. *Louise Nevelson,* 1977. Cibachrome, 16 7/8 by 15 1/3 inches. National Portrait Gallery, Smithsonian Institution/Art Resource, NY; 86, © North Carolina Museum of Art/Corbis; 91, © Estate of Fernand Léger/Artists Rights Society (ARS), NY; 94, Photo by Teresa N. Rishel, courtesy of Chihuly Studio; 95, © Museum of Fine Arts, Houston/Bridgeman Art Library; 98, © 2004 Estate of Louise Nevelson/Artists Rights Society (ARS), New York; 100, Digital image © The Museum of Modern Art/Licensed by SCALA/Art Resource, NY; 101, © David Gilhooly; 104, © Scala/Art Resource, NY; 105, © Bill Ross/Corbis; 109, Photograph © 1982 Medford Taylor/Black Star; 112(bl), © Les Orenstein; 113, Peter Yang/© Les Orenstein; 116, © Richard Cummins/Corbis; 116, © William Manning/Corbis; 116, © SuperStock; 117, © Danny Lehman/Corbis; 118, © 2004 Artists Rights

Acknowledgments

Society (ARS), New York/VG Bild Kunst, Bonn.; 119, Wassily Kandinsky. *Lady (Portrait of Gabriele Münter)*, ca. 1910. Oil on canvas, 44 by 43 1/2 inches. Munich, Lenbachhaus. Photograph © AKG London. © 2004 Wassily Kandinsky/Artists Rights Society (ARS), New York; 120, © The Tate Gallery, London/Art Resource, New York. © 2004 Succession H. Matisse, Paris/Artists Rights Society (ARS), New York; 121, © Musée Picasso, Paris/Peter Willi/SuperStock. © 2004 Estate of Pablo Picasso/Artists Rights Society (ARS), New York; 124, Digital Image © The Museum of Modern Art/Licensed by SCALA/Art Resource, NY; 125(t), Chris Gomien/Carl Solway Gallery, Cincinnati, Ohio; 128, Contact Press Images; 129, Portland Museum of Art, Portland, OR. Gift of David and Nissa Shaw. © 1970 Imogen Cunningham Trust; 132, © 2004 Artists Rights Society (ARS), New York/VG Bild Kunst, Bonn.; 133, © 2004 The Georgia O'Keeffe Foundation/Artists Rights Society (ARS), New York; 134, Photographs courtesy of the Everett Collection, Inc., New York; 139, © Helen Frankenthaler; 142, From *50 Texas Artists,* by Annette Carlozzi, © 1986, published by Chronicle Books, San Francisco. Courtesy of Chronicle Books; 146(tl), Photo by Peter Yang; 146(br), Corbis; 147, © Ralph Barrera; 150, © GoodShoot/SuperStock; 150, © Corbis; 152, Museum purchase and commission with funds from the National Endowment for the Arts, and The Benjamin J. Tillar Memorial Trust. © 2004 Red Grooms/Artists Rights Society (ARS), New York; 153, Red Grooms. *Self-Portrait as a Bus Driver,* 1998. Acrylic on paper. Palmer Museum, Pennsylvania State University, University Park, PA. © 2004 Red Grooms/Artists Rights Society (ARS), New York; 155, Photo by Parks Anderson, courtesy of Chihuly Studio; 158, Catalog Number SAR.1989-7-352, School of American Research; 159, © Kevin Fleming/Corbis; 167, © Schalkwijk/Art Resource, NY. © Fiduciario en el Fideicomiso relativo a los Museos Diego Rivera y Frida Kahlo. Reproduction authorized by the Bank of Mexico, Mexico City; 172, The Andy Warhol Foundation, Inc./Art Resource, NY. © 2004 Andy Warhol Foundation for the Visual Arts/ARS, New York; 176, © The Huntington Library, Art Collections, and Botanical Gardens, San Marino, California/SuperStock; 180(bl), © Jose Gonzalez; 181(t), 181(b), © Jose Gonzalez; 184(tc),© Paul Gilligan/Getty Images; 184, © Lynn Radeka/SuperStock; 184, © Spike Mafford/Getty Images; 186, Photo by Northern Lights, courtesy of Carmen Lomas Garza; 187, Photo © 1990 Hulleah Tsinhnahjannie, courtesy Bernice Steinbaum Gallery, Miami; 189, © Miriam Schapiro; 192, © Erich Lessing/Art Resource, NY; 193, Réunion des Musées Nationaux/Art Resource, NY; 197, © Smithsonian American Art Museum, Washington, D.C./ Art Resource, NY; 200, Photo by M. Lee Fatherree, courtesy of Carmen Lomas Garza; 202, © Smithsonian American Art Museum, Washington, D.C./Art Resource, NY; 206, Commissioned by SPARC through it's Great Walls Unlimited: Neighborhood Pride Program/Courtesy of Social and Public Art Resource Center. www.sparcmurals.org; 207, Photographed by Larry Colcher/Kansas State Historical Society; 210, © SuperStock; 211, © Steve Vidler/SuperStock; 214(b), 215 © Stan Webb; 218(tl), © Rudi Von Briel/Photoedit; 218 (tc), © Cummer Museum of Art and Gardens, Jacksonville, FL/Superstock; 218(tc), © Michael Freeman/Corbis; 218 (tr), © The Lowe Museum, The University of Miami/SuperStock.

Back Matter

Page 220, © Getty Images; 220, © Getty Images; 220, © Corbis; 220, Getty Images; 221, Getty Images; 221, digitalvisiononline.com; 222, © Darrell Gulin/Corbis; 222, © Eric Crichton/Corbis; 223, © Paul Chauncey/Corbis; 223, © Corbis; 223, © Pat Doyle/Corbis; 223, © Robert Yin/Corbis; 224, © David Frazier/Corbis; 224, © Peter Dazeley/Corbis; 224, © Richard Hamilton Smith/Corbis; 224, © Charles Gold/Corbis; 224, © Lance Nelson/Corbis; 225, © The Purcell Team/Corbis; 225, © Lindsey P. Martin/Corbis; 225, © Nik Wheeler/Corbis; 227, © Randy Faris/Corbis; 228, © Bob Krist/Corbis; 229, © Charles & Josette Lenars/Corbis; 230, © Mark Gibson/Corbis; 231, © Tom Bean/Corbis; 232, © Corbis; 233, © Getty Images; 238, © Corbis; 238, © Corbis; 239, (tl) © Corbis; 239, © Images.com/Corbis; 240, © Peter Harholdt/SuperStock; 241, © Holton Collection/SuperStock; 241, © The Lowe Art Museum, The University of Miami/SuperStock; 242, © Kim Sayer/Corbis; 243, © British Museum, London/Bridgeman Art Library, London/SuperStock; 244, © Christian Pierre/SuperStock; 245, © Roman Soumar/Corbis; 245, © Roger Allyn/SuperStock; 246, © Erik Slutsky/SuperStock; 247, © SuperStock; 248, © Corbis.